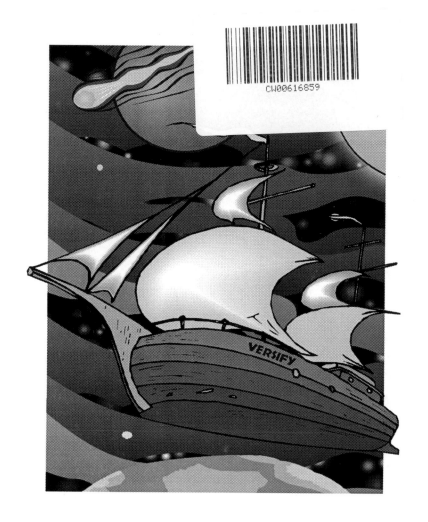

CW00616859

POETIC VOYAGES LONDON VOL III

Edited by Steve Twelvetree

To daddy & anna   2/02/02

Lots of
Love

x   x
Lucy Anne
x   x

First published in Great Britain in 2001 by
YOUNG WRITERS
Remus House,
Coltsfoot Drive,
Peterborough, PE2 9JX
Telephone (01733) 890066

Copyright Contributors 2001

HB ISBN 0 75433 386 8
SB ISBN 0 75433 387 6

FOREWORD

Young Writers was established in 1991 with the aim to promote creative writing in children, to make reading and writing poetry fun.

This year once again, proved to be a tremendous success with over 88,000 entries received nationwide.

The Poetic Voyages competition has shown us the high standard of work and effort that children are capable of today. It is a reflection of the teaching skills in schools, the enthusiasm and creativity they have injected into their pupils shines clearly within this anthology.

The task of selecting poems was therefore a difficult one but nevertheless, an enjoyable experience. We hope you are as pleased with the final selection in *Poetic Voyages London Vol III* as we are.

CONTENTS

Madeleine Wickers	80
Yoni Pakleppa	80
Felix Volhard	81
Mirella Wilson	82
Amber Tipper	83
Saul Goldblatt	84
Abbey Garrood	84
Georgia Lansdown	85
Jamie Adams	85
Ayesha Chinn	86
James Simpson	86
Martha Young	87
Oliver De Wan	87
Imogen Rance	88
Georgia Anderson	88
Ziggy Hasan	89
Tom Hatherley	89
Sean Wilkinson	90
Aimee MacKenzie	90
Hannah Johnson	91
Matthew McLoughlin	91
Imogen Buxton	92
Nima Toserkani	92
Thomas Glover	93
Lottie Guy	93
Emerald A Robertson-Rose	94
Nathan Travers	94
Clara Baldock	95
Caitlin Boswell-Jones	95
Louis Marsh	96
Ben Gilbert	96
Alexandra Karavias	97
Rachel Weekes	97
Jessica Louise Pitts Brennan	98
Michael Simpson	98
Saskia Harrison	99
Chinua Phinn-Archer	99
Alice Clara Engelhard	100

The Poems

THE RIVERS OF JUPITER

Calmly cruising through the rivers of Jupiter,
Admiring its bubbly waters,
Flamboyantly floating in its mystic presence,
Still smoothly floating on.

Going nowhere where the rivers wouldn't take me,
Just staring into space,
Drifting slowly on and on,
Still smoothly floating on.

I was sailing through the reddish rivers,
I was staring to see what I could find,
I was floating in a fantasy world,
By now you've probably guessed it,
It was all in my mind.

Billy Senington (11)
Deansfield Primary School

MY POETIC VOYAGE

I would love to travel to the time of Camelot,
I would like to peer at the waterside,
See the enchanted blue waters,
What lies beyond the walls of the castle?
I would love to know why willows whiten, aspens quiver,
Surrounding the bewitched castle of Shalott.
Where's the Lady of Shalott?
Why does she die?

Shaun Smith (10)
Deansfield Primary School

THE CHEETAH

I'm sprinting across the boiling desert,
I'm a cheetah.
I'm jumping across a wet jungle,
I'm a cheetah.
I'm springing across stormy seas,
I'm a cheetah.
I'm galloping across green grass,
I'm a cheetah.
I'm dashing across vast fields,
I'm a cheetah.
I'm scuttering across silky ice,
I'm a cheetah.

Daniel Wakefield (10)
Deansfield Primary School

MY FANTASTIC JOURNEY

My journey begins . . .
Walking on stairs that never end.
Cars that fly through the air.
Swimming in the water.
Jump back to the time of the Egyptians.
Fall off the white dome.
Land in a pool of lava.
Fly fast like an aeroplane.
Dive down to Atlantis.
Eat all the oyster shells in the deepest water.
But my journey will never end.

Daniella Dorothy (10)
Deansfield Primary School

MY VOYAGE ON THE TRAMPOLINE

I opened the door and fell furiously,
It was pitch-black,
Then I saw light green,
I landed and bounced back up in the air,
It was like I was on a trampoline.

The trampoline fell and kept falling into a room,
It was a cave,
It felt like I was being watched,
I kept on falling into different rooms,
Then I woke.

Claire Donovan (10)
Deansfield Primary School

MY MOST MAGICAL TRIP

I would love to . . .

Fly with no wings.
Walk on this air.
Skate down from the highest mountain.
Jump into an unknown kingdom.
Walk on water, scurrying fast.
Bungee-jump with no strings.
Slide on Saturn's rings.
Sunbathe on the bottom of the sea.
Meet the penguins on top of the sun.
Jump out of a plane into a pool.

Portia Graham (10)
Deansfield Primary School

JOURNEY THROUGH MY IMAGINATION

In my imagination
I opened the door, I was whisked away.
I was in a typhoon, it blew me to the bottom of the sea.
Its golden reefs alive like ours above,
The rainbow fish glide round the reef.

In my imagination
I fly to the solar system, I land on Mercury.
I will melt if I'm here for too long,
So I jump to Venus, this brilliant world.
Then to Earth, our home planet.
I jumped through the solar system,
This three dimension world.

Toby Hubbard (10)
Deansfield Primary School

THE JOURNEY WITH THE SWAN

Snow gently tickling my cheeks,
wings of the swan proudly flapping,
a blanket of snow covers the world
like butter spread over the ground.

Stars are twinkling in the sky,
as the swan flaps gracefully by,
I feel the warmth of its beautiful wings
and my hair ruffles back in the wind.

Hannah Weston (11)
Deansfield Primary School

MY VOYAGE

I open the door, milkshake drifting around me
Fizzing and changing ways.
Dogs licking me on my favourite book,
Dancing on the waves.
I look, a waterfall appearing,
I start to shiver with fear - *stop!*

Everything around me is quiet.
No more gushing milkshake but a rainbow stream
Taking me where I want to go.

Little gummi bears dancing around in a circle,
Singing to a peaceful tune.
The tune getting lower and lower.
Then *bang!* I woke up on the warmth of my carpet.

Claire Gosling (11)
Deansfield Primary School

JACK, THE TYPICAL CAT

Jack is a family cat.
It's surprising he's not really fat.
If he's not catching birds he is eating a mouse
Or begging for food in the house.
When he's not eating he is asleep on a bed.
He likes it in the garden climbing trees.
Although sometimes he gets fleas,
This means he scratches all day long,
But in his family's eyes he can do no wrong.

Lucy Whyte (6)
Deansfield Primary School

MY VOYAGE

Opening this wooden door I see:
An underwater world.
I hear the swish of a dolphin's tail,
And feel the sinking of sand underfoot.
Seeing a crowd of wispy seaweed
I proceed.

Beyond this seaweed door I see:
A field of endless sky.
I hear the flap of a tired bird's wings,
And feel the softness of a cotton wool cloud.
Seeing a crowd of flying geese
I proceed.

Opening this fluffy door I see:
A dense, overgrown forest.
I hear the chirp of a nearby parrot,
And feel the softness of a monkey's tail.
Seeing a clearing
I proceed.

Stepping through this clearing I see:
A comforting room around me.
I hear the hum of a radiator,
And feel the weight of a patterned blanket.
Seeing the end of a wonderful dream
I wake up,
And wish I could proceed.

Rebecca Luxton (11)
Deansfield Primary School

THE MAGICAL LAND

I found a door in my room one night
I walked right through
I flew through tubes
It was like a rollercoaster
Then finally I got to the mysterious land
I realised I was on Saturn
I span around on his rings for hours
Then I saw a head popping out from Saturn
It said, 'What's the noise?'
'Oh hello,' I said
We started talking for a billion years
Well, OK it was only 2 minutes
'Will I ever get home?' I said
I saw a lot of tubes
I followed them around the hole
I jumped in one of the chairs
And got blasted through the sky
The next thing I knew I was in my own bed
I thought, 'Was it a dream?'

Natalie Sharp (10)
Deansfield Primary School

TRAVELLING

When I close my eyes
I'm a leaf swaying through the air
Riding on a squirrel's back
Travelling through anywhere
Scared of the bee behind me
But someone calls, I have to open my eyes.

Tom Cook (10)
Deansfield Primary School

PIZZA PALACE

A palace made out of cheery cheese
People made out of pepper and pepperoni
How I wish I could take a huge bite.
Then I look up to see a sign made out of tomato
Saying *Pizza Kingdom.*

I look over my shoulder to see a small town
Of margherita houses. Y*um! Yum!*
A whiff of pepper and margherita fills my nose
My mouth starts to water
Next thing I know it is *crunch!*
I've taken a bite from the ground.

The stringy cheese starts flowing down my throat
It tastes delicious
I can't help myself
I bite off a corner of the tomato sign
It tastes sweet and juicy.

Esther Burns (9)
Deansfield Primary School

MY JOURNEY

I would love to . . .

Have a sauna in the middle of Mars.
See dolphins jumping over the moon.
Walk on thin air.
Fly without wings.
To see penguins dancing on the sun.
Jump out of a cloud filled with water.
Leap into an unknown kingdom.

Lilly May Watson (10)
Deansfield Primary School

POETIC VOYAGES

I walk up the staircase
With a slow and steady pace
But what do I see there?
A secret door with a stair.

A stair that says, 'Come here
And you'll find secrets here my dear.'
So I unlock the door
And out pours . . .

A mound of dogs,
Then some frogs
That start to swirl my way
And then I start to sway.

I end up in the Caribbean
The fit boys you should see 'em!
I should go home now
My daydream it was *wow!*

Lauren McNulty (10)
Deansfield Primary School

MY FAVOURITE JOURNEY

I stepped into the future
In the magical coach,
I cut a mighty massive hole,
Through the midnight
I'm floating in an exotic bubble
Sinking in the icy Atlantic Ocean
Touching a frozen iceberg
My journey ends here
When I am asleep.

Sirin Ustaoglu (10)
Deansfield Primary School

MY VOYAGE TO THE MILKY WAY

I opened the fridge door,
To get a chocolate,
Then I was sucked in,
I swirled and twirled,
And I fell through the Milky Way.

I opened my eyes,
And there I was,
Floating in the air,
Surrounded by Milky Ways.

It was my dream,
And it came true,
But I'll never go back,
Through the fridge door.

Aimee Copley (10)
Deansfield Primary School

MY JOURNEY

I like to . . .

Drive on thin air,
build an igloo on lava,
scurry across space as a black spider,
swim on freezing ice.

I would love to surf on a shooting star,
walk on cold water,
fly with bird wings,
ski on the sun while eating a sun cream.

Craig Nixon (10)
Deansfield Primary School

THE DAY I CLOSED MY EYES

The day I closed my eyes,

I fell through a letterbox as swiftly as I could,
Then through a whirlpool of ideas and curiosity.

The day I closed my eyes,

I fell into a never-ending fall,
Then through the sun's core,
Burning my skin a golden bronze.

The day I closed my eyes,

I fell through a never-ending star gaze,
As I drown into different forms.

The day I closed my eyes,

I was swimming through the Niagara falls,
Swooping round the pyramids of Giza.

Josh Roberts (11)
Deansfield Primary School

MY JOURNEY

I would love to . . .

Slide down Saturn's rings,
Jump off the highest mountain,
When I'm about to hit the ground,
Float above the London Eye,
Dance with a baby monkey,
Swim with a leaping dolphin,
Run like a tiger.

Carys Gale (10)
Deansfield Primary School

THE SPACEMAN

When I looked out of my window
I saw the planet Mars
Before I looked out of my window
My room was full of chocolate bars.

Then I flew up into space
And I landed on Mars
I had a bag full
Of chocolate bars.

When I fell I landed on my sister's face
Which was a funny place.

Jak Thomas (6)
Deansfield Primary School

MY MAGICAL VOYAGE

If only I could fly without wings,
Slide on Saturn's rocky rings.
Or maybe I could stay as a child,
Fall off the tallest mountain.

What if I could travel in space,
And build an igloo on cold Pluto.
Or swim in hot lava,
And jump in cool, cold ice cream.

That would be my dream journey.

Nicola Jones (10)
Deansfield Primary School

I WENT INTO SPACE

I made a rocket in May
and I made it in one day.
I used some metal for the bottom
and I used some cotton.

I went up to space
and I saw a funny face,
it was quite a disgrace.

In the rocket
I had a great big pocket
and in that pocket
there was a socket.

I went back to Earth
and my mum gave birth
to a little alien called Adrian.

Elliot Behan (7)
Deansfield Primary School

SURF IN SPACE

I would like to surf in space
like a star.

I would like to surf in space
at top speed.

I would like to surf in space
and meet living life on the moon.

Daniel Phillips (10)
Deansfield Primary School

DREAMY VOYAGE

I close my eyes,
And drift to lands far away,
From India to Russia.
I see many multitudes,
Great and small.

Many crowds,
From England to Canada,
From Switzerland to Fairyland.
I drift and float,
I blow away to . . .
Thought Land.

Tomi Owolabi (10)
Deansfield Primary School

IN THE JUNGLE

When I closed my eyes
I was on a tiger's back
Riding, riding
See a monkey swing
Swinging, swinging
Look at a camel spit
Spitting, spitting
Watch a bird cruise by
Cruising, cruising
Hear a parrot echo me
Echo me, echo me!

Shaun Wilkin (10)
Deansfield Primary School

PARADISE

My imagination has taken me to a place where . . .

I had grown wings and I was sitting on a cloud
With silence all around me.

I sat there feeling free from a complicated life.

My head felt as clear as the sky
On a hot summer's morning.

I heard nothing, nothing at all,
Not even birds fluttering their wings below me.

Tommy Cunningham (10)
Deansfield Primary School

MY JOURNEY

There I was sitting on the sandy shore.
The strong breeze was blowing in my face.
I was drinking a cocktail.

Swimming in the sea.
Lucky old me.
Seeing the fish float by.

I build sandcastles in the sand.
I then sit and watch a band.
I really enjoyed this journey

Clare Freeman (11)
Deansfield Primary School

WHERE AM I?

I fell through the floorboards
I landed in a heap on the floor
I had landed in a strange room
Where there were lots of strange things
Tables, chairs, TVs and plants
Big things, smelly things
Little furniture, big furniture.

I felt funny and bubbly inside
I heard strange sounds in the background
A sound like people rushing around like factory machines.

The room looked clean and the tables were shining
It smelt fresh like a field of daffodils .
The noise in the background was getting louder and louder
I started to feel strange
I sat down and there I was in a strange world.

The room was big
There were two doors each side of the room
The door on the left side was the door
Where the noises were coming from
I was still feeling funny and strange inside.

Lucy Elliott (8)
Deansfield Primary School

A BOY WENT UP TO SPACE

One day a boy went up to space
He brought his suitcase
He saw lots of shooting stars
One shooting star was going to Mars.

The boy landed on Mars
He saw some aliens but they looked like stars
The aliens were mean
So he went home for dinner.

Charles Parker (6)
Deansfield Primary School

MY VOYAGE

As I opened the French windows,
I was blinded by vivid colours,
Reds, yellows, blues and greens.
I stood,
I stared,
I blinked,
And I blinked again.
A brilliant blue sun.
A great green sky.
What is this artificial life?
A vibrant violet vulture swooped past,
I close my eyes,
I take a step back,
I trip,
I open my eyes,
I wasn't surrounded by bright colours,
I was surrounded by dull colours,
Greys, blacks and browns.
At this first sight,
I knew where I was,
Home again.

Lucy Burrluck (11)
Deansfield Primary School

AGE OF EMPIRES THREE

As if by magic my computer went red,
Sucked me in then my bed!
I fell down the monitor, thought I was dead.
I landed in a heap and hit my head.
I stood up, I thought I was in a game called 'You Can't Kill Me'.
But then I realised I was in Age Of Empires Three.

A man stepped out of the mist and said, 'Come with me.'
I didn't know what to do. 'Who are you?' I asked.
No reply.
I followed the man
Into a house like a frying pan!
'I want to go home,' I said to him.
'No!' cried the man, 'The sentry's army is quite dim.'

Then he took me to the castle
And gave me a parcel.
I opened it rapidly to find some armour.
'Go out and fight the evil bats,' said the farmer.
'I don't know how to fight,
I have no might.'
'I'll teach you how.'

'When?' 'Right now.'
The farmer took me to his king
'Kill a dragon or a monster thing!
Then you can join in big bad, battle of all time.'
'Did you realise I am talking in rhyme?' said the king
'Just go out and kill that monster thing.'

I walked along sadly.
I wanted to go home badly.
Then I saw a microchip.
All I had to do was make the chip go zip!
I pulled the plug.
I really felt like I had taken a drug.
I was pulled off my feet.
I was getting back to my time, what a treat.

I woke up in bed
My face bright red
Only a dream
What a scene!

Glenn Ifield (9)
Deansfield Primary School

MY IMAGINARY WORLD POEM

Dark, shadowy, smelly and silent.
Then, *whooo!*
I hit a switch,
Suddenly bright, dazzling, shining.
Hot, burning, scorching!
I walk forward.
A brilliant, blinding, portal in front of me.
Zap!
Whoosh!
I'm home!

Louis Youpa (9)
Deansfield Primary School

SWEETIE LAND

I got sucked into a sweetie box,
I landed in a pile of leaves,
But when I looked round and round,
All I saw were sweeties.

When I got up,
I stood upon my feet,
I looked round and saw people
And all they did was eat.

I wanted to have some,
So I got a lolly,
But I didn't eat it, so I can prove it,
To my friend Holly.

In front of me was a cottage,
I opened the door,
I took a step inside
And chocolate was the floor.

Suddenly, there was a quick flash of light,
Then I saw a chocolate fox,
I closed my eyes and took another step
And I was out of the box.

Sanel Kaplan (9)
Deansfield Primary School

I LOOKED OUT MY WINDOW

I looked out my window
Late one night
Although it was very dark
It was an amazing sight.

The moon shone down
With its yellow light
Twinkling all around
Were stars shining bright.

Matthew Theobald (6)
Deansfield Primary School

SWEET DREAMS

It was a terrible noise
A deafening noise
A horrible noise
From my bedroom
My beautiful room
It was my horse
My horse painting
My high-flying horse painting
I stroked my high-flying horse painting
I was sucked in my high-flying horse painting
I was flying
I fell through a gingerbread-built house

On a gingerbread-built table
An orange jelly baby
He was riding a spider
He took me to a bug shop
And got me a praying mantis
He led me to a gingerbread house
My garden was beautiful
Chocolate trees
And milkshake lakes of all kinds

Hannah Luxton (8)
Deansfield Primary School

MY VOYAGE

The hole was deep, deeper than ever,
I hit the water, waded to the shore.

The shore was hard, harder than ever,
I hopped to the door.

The handle was hot, hotter than ever,
I dropped into the wind.

The wind was fast, faster than ever,
I reached out to the sea.

The sea was choppy, more choppy than ever,
I swam to the wreck.

The wreck was cosy, cosier than ever,
My mind was unable.

My mind was unable, more unable than ever,
To go back.

To go back was hard, harder than ever,
I found myself.

I found myself dreaming, dreaming more than ever,
The sad thing was.

The sad thing was sadder than ever,
I lost touch with my voyage.

Marissa Arrows (10)
Deansfield Primary School

SWEET LAND

I'm in a strange tunnel,
The walls are squidgy.
There's thick, scrumptious jam, it's very sticky.
This tunnel is dark,
It's a Swiss roll tunnel

Outside it smells sweet,
I think it smells like toffee.
There's all sorts of things here,
Chocolate, candyfloss, marzipan.

I can see jelly baby people,
Red, green, pink, yellow
And lots more.
They're very small,
They're as small as mice.

There are fluffy marshmallow clouds,
They are soft and squidgy,
Soft as feathers.

I can't hear anything,
It's silent.
All I can hear is the quiet flap of birds' wings.
It's as silent as an empty road.

Olivia Bennett (9)
Deansfield Primary School

MY VOYAGE

I opened the door of many colours,
To see that I was under the sea.
I was falling, falling, falling to the bottom of the sea.
Swirling and whirling in the deep blue sea.
A choir of dolphins, floating in a circle around me.

I slept on a dolphin, it was very slippery,
The colours of red, blue, green and yellow surrounding me,
Everywhere I floated,
I swooped in and out the seaweed, around fishes swimming in a group.
It was as clear as the air brushing around me.

I thought I was dreaming,
It proved me wrong,
As the sharks sang, the sea horses played their instruments.

They let me go, I floated all the way, to the top of the sea.
White dusk sparkling around me, I stepped to the door of many colours,
I opened it, and
   skipped through.

Stephanie Asbury (10)
Deansfield Primary School

THE CLOUDS OF MERCURY

Smoky steam rises into the wispy clouds of Mercury.

I drift in the scorching air as sunbeams blaze through the hazy clouds.

I glide on the lava orange breeze
That floats gently above the fiery planet of Mercury.

I watch boiling bubbling lava under the misty cloudy sky.

Nathan Aspell (11)
Deansfield Primary School

SKYLAND

A city in the sky. Far beyond the clouds,
With hovercraft gliding through the air.

Emerald-shaped islands floating up so high,
With rocket-powered jetpacks they zoom around.
Bridges join the islands together.

The buildings are tall like giraffes or beanstalks reaching for the clouds.

Eagles watch from trees, looking out for predators.

They swoop down, claws at the ready to attack their prey
And bring it back to their hungry chicks.

Max Davis (9)
Deansfield Primary School

I'M IN THE SEA GOING DOWN

I'm in the sea going down, down, down.
I'm swimming with the dolphins going down, down, down.
The sea horses tickling my toes going down, down, down.
The mermaids sitting on the rocks are watching.
I'm laughing but somehow I'm feeling sad.
It's a wonderful feeling under the sea.

I'm floating up towards the surface.
I'm home.
It was wonderful under the sea.

Rosie Ashley (8)
Deansfield Primary School

THE JOURNEY INTO SPACE

I went into space one day
On the way I saw the Milky Way.

I saw the glittery stars
And the big red Mars.

I stopped at Mars to see the stars
And I ate some chocolate bars.

I got into my rocket
And put the key in my pocket.

I got into my rocket and I went home
And then I went to see the dome.

Samantha Deman (6)
Deansfield Primary School

ESCAPE TO SPACE

I broke my rocket when it was May,
So I'm going to make another one today,
I was putting on a top and it went pop!

I went up to space where I saw a race,
We had a picnic and she nicked it!
I tripped over the moon and got hot,
It was noon and fell in a cot.

I sewed my bottom with cotton,
Dad said, 'What's on your bottom?'
And I said, 'It's cotton.'

Dean Atkins (6)
Deansfield Primary School

THE MAN'S JOURNEY

Once a man went up to space,
he saw the planets on the way.
He flew in his brand new rocket,
and saw the Milky Way.

He went to visit Mars,
he did not like Mars.
He saw Jupiter, Mercury and Venus,
so went to the stars and loved the stars.

Then he heard his mother shout,
did he like his journey out?
He promised to come back,
then he went all the way home.

Samuel Llewellyn (6)
Deansfield Primary School

A JOURNEY TO SPACE

I went to space and saw my face
Then I saw the Milky Way
I floated near Mars and saw the stars
And ate chocolate bars.

I saw Jupiter too, I love it more
Than Mars and the stars too
I met an alien, it was pink and it was fluffy
I ran because it was nearly May.

Then I saw Venus, that was best, I say.

Ellen Harmsworth (6)
Deansfield Primary School

SWEETIE LAND

I saw Maltesers shaped like tennis balls on the roofs,
I saw massive, smooth vanilla ice cream,
I saw cars made of liquorice strings,
I loved it, I loved it, I loved it, I loved it!

The Maltesers tasted great!
The ice cream tasted fab!
The cars tasted wonderful!
I loved it, I loved it, I loved it, I loved it!

I lived in sweets,
The roof was made of Maltesers,
The path was made of Curlywurlys,
I loved it, I loved it, I loved it, I loved it!

I loved it,
I loved it,
I loved it,
I loved it.

Laura Atkins (9)
Deansfield Primary School

THE SPACE RACE

I went to space for a race
I jumped out of my spaceship
What a disgrace!
I landed on Mars
The stars were shining
On the chocolate bars.

Joseph O'Rourke (6)
Deansfield Primary School

PLAY AWAY

On a bright sunny day
I came out to play
Walking and talking through the sun
Hey what fun!

Nearby trees were blowing
Many dads their lawns were mowing
Onto my bike I jumped
And over the curb I bumped.

And my journey to the park
I saw two dogs, did they bark!
Journey's end! Lo and behold
We had to run, run and run because it was cold.

I played all day
Until the sky was grey.
Then home I went
To my home in Kent!

Samuel James Smith (9)
Deansfield Primary School

MY VOYAGE

I stepped out of the door,
into . . . space,
colours, swirling,
stars, twinkling,
sun, gleaming,
Saturn's rings, swirling.

Laura King (10)
Deansfield Primary School

MY VOYAGE

I open the door, I'm bumping,
I look down, there is nothing,
Just white as paper.

I'm on a sailing boat,
And there's a window waiting for me!

I go in
   I'm
      floating
        I'm
          flying

I look down, I see myself playing,
I try to work it out,
I'm up here, I've got
   butterfly
       wings, red, orange and blue.
I open the door, I look,
I'm on a yellow rubby ducky, floating back home.
Whirling
   in
     a
      pattern.

Donna Gardner (10)
Deansfield Primary School

A LITTLE GIRL IN SPACE

I went to space
And my name is Grace.
I made a rocket one day
That was in May.
I saw some aliens
And they said I looked like a stadium.

I saw some stars
I saw Mars
And I saw the Milky Way
And I went back for tea
And said, 'Whoopee!'

Grace Agambar (7)
Deansfield Primary School

I AM ME

I am sleepy, dreamy
While I am dreaming of the unicorn.

I ride the silver, glittering unicorn
To many different places.

Every night I see the sight
Of many happy faces.

We always go somewhere special,
We always have a laugh,
Every night in my dreams.

I always smile in my dreams
Because the unicorn is there.

We go around the planets,
We sail on the seven seas,
Wherever I want to go she will take me to,
Even if it is underwater,
She will go down like I wanted to.

When I hear a funny ringing in my ears
The unicorn magically fades away into the sun,
But I know she will always be back again tonight.

Hayley Jane Pain (8)
Deansfield Primary School

THE SHIP TO PARADISE

Far and wide we travelled to get there,
The huge great waves and the strong salty air.

Oh what a beautiful place so fair and grand,
You can feel the hot sun as you walk on the sand.

The air is so sweet and the sky is so blue,
You can feel the hot beaming sun shining down on you.

As the moon comes up and the sun seems to die,
You walk along the shore and look up at the sky.

'What a great time,' you hear yourself say,
One amazing place and a brilliant day.

Elyse Pearce (8)
Deansfield Primary School

THE SHIP TO NEVER LAND

Over the hills and far away,
A ship is sailing along this day,
To a place called Never Land behind the mountains,
Where you admire the trees and fountains.

As you walk across the sand,
I've never seen a place so grand,
To get there you have to travel so far,
You need something better than a speedy car.

Over the hills and far away,
A ship is sailing along this day.

Josie Senington (8)
Deansfield Primary School

THE TRIP UNDER THE SEA

I jumped into it and down, down, down, really deep.
I swam with the fish twirling and whirling.
I watched as the killer whales swam around me.
I was twisting and turning.
Sea horses tickling me.
The wonderful mermaids performed a dance.
I swam among the shipwrecks.
My friends had put on a parade.
They handed me a fish as a gift.
I climbed onto the dolphin's back.
He took me back to shore.

Was it a dream or not?

Sara Richards (8)
Deansfield Primary School

WINTER

Soft white snow
Gleaming in the moonlight
Like a cold white blanket
Spread across the ground
Sparkling snowflakes glistening in the trees
Winter so beautiful
Trees all bare
Robins singing sweet soothing songs
And tiny bird footprints
In the lovely snow.

Holly Chisnell (9)
Deansfield Primary School

SKY LAND

Sky Land, so wonderful and magical,
A faint milky sky, showers of golden stars,
Sky Land, so wonderful and magical.

So colourful and shiny, everything's a dream,
Moons, so many moons, all different shapes and sizes,
Sky Land, so wonderful and magical.

Puffy, fluffy white clouds,
I feel as though I can fly!
Sky Land, so wonderful and magical.

I smell a soft, sweet, tempting smell,
Like candy at the fair.
Sky Land, so wonderful and magical.

Bright, magic planets, greens, purples and blues!
I'm having so much fun.
Sky Land, so wonderful and magical!

Daisy Taylor (9)
Deansfield Primary School

SAILING ON THE SEA

I was sailing on the sea
I felt a draught blowing on me.
It was so cold it made me quiver
And I gave a little shiver.
I was entering the bottom of the sea
I didn't drown
Like it was supposed to be.
I swam and swam like you'll never believe
What I swam in was like an ocean made from cheese!

Richard Griggs (8)
Deansfield Primary School

I AM A DOLPHIN

I am blue and glittery.
I sparkle when the sun shines on me.
I hate it when people have rides on me.
I like kind and gentle people.
I was brought here when I was two.
I like to be trained.
I am very polite to everyone.
I love to be washed.
I like it where I live because it is hot.
A kind man gives me food.
He gives me fish.
I live with other dolphins.
One day they brought me back to the sea.
The sharks are in the sea.
I got bitten by a big black shark.
They took me to a cold and wet place.
It was a big adventure.

Lucy-Anne Castelino (8)
Deansfield Primary School

FRUTIE TUTIE CANDY LAND

Frutie Tutie Candy Land
Sweets, fruit, candy
Sweet-smelling toffee apples
Candy cans sweet for your sweet tooth
Drinks from delicious milkshakes
Brown chocolate tree trunks
Strawberry-headed people
Every sweet and fruit that fills your head
To make your tongue and mouth water.

Daisy Victoria Brand (9)
Deansfield Primary School

DRAGON ADVENTURE

My name is Dragon.
I am a green dragon.
Dragon is my name.
I have shiny green scales on my back.
I live in a scary cave.
I breathe flames to scare my enemies.
I go out of my cave and fall through a secret trap door.
An ugly hunter comes from behind a tree full of leaves.
He takes me to North America.
The hunter sells me to a circus for lots of money.
I crept out of the circus
Past the thicket to the open land.
I journeyed back home.
Miles away from the circus.
I saw an army march by.
A sign said
'8 million dollar reward
For the person who catches this dragon.'
The picture on the sign was me.
One army soldier was carrying some suits.
I walked quietly behind him.
I took one of them.
I put on the suit.
I joined the rest of the army.
The army walked past a ship.
It was about to leave.
I got on the ship.
I went to England.
The ship stopped at a harbour right by my house.

Alex Goodman (8)
Deansfield Primary School

UNDERWATER LAND

Fishes, fishes, fishes
In Underwater Land
Swimming, swimming, swimming
In Underwater Land

People, people, people
In Underwater Land
Surfing, surfing, surfing on boards
So smart and grand

People and fishes friends there
In Underwater Land
Parties, parties, parties
In Underwater Land

It smells like chlorine
In Underwater Land
The surfboards they ride on are shimmering and coloured
In Underwater Land

The fishes in the sea dart about like arrows
They're also bright and colourful
In Underwater Land
The big ones eat the nasty ones
In Underwater Land

The water there is shimmering blue
Like dolphins in their deep blue pool
In Underwater Land

I'd really love to live there
In Underwater Land

Katy Taylor (9)
Deansfield Primary School

EVERYTHING STAYS BLUE

The ship left the port
Sailing on and on.
It was very odd, very.
Everything was blue, everything.
Blue, blue and more blue.
The trees were light blue and so were the sheep in the field.
My voyage stopped. I got out. It was my hotel.
It was also blue, bold blue.
I got inside; that also was a wonderful light blue.
The receptionist was a darker blue than everything else was.
I went to my room, also blue.
I need to get a drink but I can't find a door because it's *blue!*

Rachel Young (9)
Deansfield Primary School

CANDY LAND

Candy Land's a dream chocolate ice cream on the ground
Dark chocolate buttons all around
Jelly babies walking and talking - what a sight!
Jelly babies are tasty
I tried to get one but they are too bright.
The jelly babies are huge, the size of a house
Brown gloomy gingerbread houses on the left
Pond in the corner tastes like strawberry
Houses taste like chocolate and banana, *yum, yum.*
Goodbye Candy Land, I will come back soon.

Anthony Tatman (9)
Deansfield Primary School

I AM A PILOT

Hey, my name is Alex.
I have a very big aeroplane.
I fly through the sky.
Higher and higher I go.
It's a wonderful sight to see.
Up there so high, higher and higher I go.
I see lots of other aeroplanes too.
Mine's the best.
I go to other places, the best one was the jungle.
The trees are scary and hairy,
Gloomy caves all dark and scary.
Monkeys jumping around and around.
I saw some tigers, that freaked me out.

Alex Webb (8)
Deansfield Primary School

I AM A FAIRY

I am a fairy called Sally
I have beautiful, glittery wings
I have white and creamy shoes
I have coloured hair bands
I eat lots of fruit and veg
I make people happy when they're upset
I like beautiful little children too
In the amazing blue sky
I do secret things in there
To make the world better.

Behice Kaplan (8)
Deansfield Primary School

IMAGINE

Imagine sailing through
Civilisation and unknown galaxies
Till
You're sailing through a black atmosphere
Only passing air
Then only passing colour
Rainbows are being made
Rushing colour
Burning bright
The stars are marking
The start of night
Seeing planets
Sparkle in the silvery light
Now the moon is up
It marks the start of night
The moon and stars
In the silvery light
Imagine.

Grace Bradshaw (9)
Deansfield Primary School

MY SHIP

My ship went sailing out to sea,
It left the port at steady speed.
Once at sea the waves were high,
In the distance they touched the sky.
This is where I want to be,
Sailing forever on the sea.

Joe Hagan (9)
Deansfield Primary School

I AM A FAIRY

I'm a fairy up in the sky.
My name is Butterfly.
I'm no ordinary fairy.
I'm a tooth fairy.
My dress is purple.
My hair is golden.
I have blue eyes.
I do like to sing.
I do like to dance
But best of all I like to travel.
Today I flew down a drainpipe.
I met a spider who was hiding something.
Just a key to open a cupboard where money is hidden.
I opened the cupboard.
Inside was money.
We shared the money and now we are friends
And we sang and danced and we weaved together.

Hayley Lewis (8)
Deansfield Primary School

LAND OF CHOCOLATE

As I walked through the door the captain said,
'Land of Chocolate, stopping here, Land of Chocolate.'
Land of Chocolate I'm on my way
I am in for an amazing day
Gooey and sticky and yummy too
I love chocolate
How about you?

Robert Crouch (8)
Deansfield Primary School

THE SKY

Here I am in the sky
Floating in the clouds
The clouds are white, fluffy and huge
Like a pile of feathers soft and smooth.

I'm sliding down the rainbow
Full of different colours to see
In the sky I can see the birds flap their wings.

I can smell the fresh air rushing past me
The sun is blazing in the sky as bright as can be.

Then I hear the alarm go off
I look around and see there's nothing else
Except for me.

Yasemin Olcusenler (9)
Deansfield Primary School

JOURNEY TO SCHOOL

A big backpack on my back
I have forgotten my PE kit
I am sad

Pencil case in my bag
Lots of food in my lunchbox
I look at the mud on my shoes

It's a rush
And lots of puff
I wish I had never gone to school

It's my birthday
I hope I'm not too late.

Tony Antoniou (7)
Deansfield Primary School

I Am A Diver

I am a deep sea diver
I dive into the icy cold sea
I catch fish for my dinner
Something caught my eye
It was a spooky old pirate ship
I slowly swam over to it
I crept inside
My heart was beating fast
I saw a wooden box
I opened it
Inside it was full of shining treasure
Gold, silver, gleaming coins
Sparkling crown jewels
I took the old box to the surface
And I became a millionaire

Daniel Parker (7)
Deansfield Primary School

I Am A Mermaid

I like waggling my beautiful tail.
I live in the sea in a castle.
I swam to the beach to get some pearls.
I saw something.
I went over to it, it was a ship.
I got stuck in a net.
I chewed myself out.
So I carried on to the beach.
I got there, I picked up some pearls.
I went home.

Katie Morris (7)
Deansfield Primary School

I Am A Robin

I am a robin
My name is Lucky.
I like worms
But apples are yucky.
I usually eat tasty worms a lot
When I fly to India it's very hot.
Bright water is the best
I have long feathers and a red chest.
I went on an adventure to India.
I flew to a town in India
Then I saw a sign, it said
'End of the line'.
So I flew through the trees
Landed on my knees.
I saw a magic worm
It started to squirm.
I made a wish
Flickered like a fish.
Then I found myself at home
With the squirming worm.
To my amazement I saw one hundred worms
All nice and raw.
Some squirming worms behind them.

Alice Martin (8)
Deansfield Primary School

The Centre Of The Earth

I was drifting down and down,
My body straight as a pin,
Twirling and twisting,
My face blowing back,
The water flying up.

I hit the middle of the Earth,
Looking around I listened to the blowing winds,
I stood up,
Still in my trunks I walked,
I was damp,
And could feel the coldness.

Adam Middleton (9)
Deansfield Primary School

I AM A CHINESE DRAGON

I am sparkly.
I am multicoloured.
I made a nail clipper
Out of sparkly shells.
I live near a sparkly beach.
My teeth are sparkly white.
I live in a gold mansion.
My right wing is red.
My left wing is orange.
My teeth are very sharp.
I drink Lucozade.
I eat ginger wheat and pie.
I am going on a journey.
I am going to a rainforest.
I am going to meet monkeys,
I'll feed them bananas.
I am on my journey in the rainforest.
It is tipping down.
There is lots of mud.
I feel like jumping into it.
Ow! Ouch! Something hard is in this mud.
Gold and two bananas.

Madeline Chase (7)
Deansfield Primary School

I AM A MERMAID

I am a mermaid,
My name is Twinkle,
I live in the lovely wavy sea,
In a beautiful stone castle.
I have shiny beautiful scales,
I am voyaging into a cave,
To find a baby sea horse.
I made a bed for her with purple shells.

I told her that I too have beautiful shiny scales.
I put the baby sea horse to bed.
An evil, horrid octopus came.
As she saw me,
She swiftly swam away.

I took the sea horse where the evil, horrid octopus would not find her,
In the flowers.
But then the evil, horrid octopus kidnapped the baby sea horse.
Next morning the baby sea horse had gone.
I went to find her.
I found a glass bottle with a letter inside,
I read the letter.
'You will find the sea horse in the octopuses cave'.
The octopus slept,
I took the sea horse back to the flowers to play,
We played all day.

Gracie Copley (7)
Deansfield Primary School

I AM A PARROT

I am a parrot called Rosie
My feathers are red as can be.
I've got a golden yellow beak
And eyes like the sea.
I went on a voyage one day.
Up, up I flew.
I saw a blue box.
Down, down I flew.
I opened the box.
There it was - a magic stone,
Laying there on a pink pillow.
I picked it up and made a wish.
To my surprise, there I was, back at home
Eating a delicious bowl of pears.

Hannah Parker (8)
Deansfield Primary School

RABBIT TRAIL

I saw a little rabbit
He was jumping on a door
I fell down the door
And landed in a jaw
As I fell down
I saw a crown
Lying on the floor
I landed in my bed
When I was meant to be on the floor
What a strange day I've had
Where was I all day long?

Alexandra Burrows (8)
Deansfield Primary School

I AM TARZAN

I live in a tree house
I am a kind of monkey
I was adopted by a monkey
Can you believe that?

My mum had died
I have to eat leaves
The worst thing of all
Was when I was swinging from tree to tree

I slipped and fell down
I broke my leg
I have lots of monkey friends
They didn't slip once

Michael Kenny (7)
Deansfield Primary School

TARZAN

I am Tarzan
I am famous
I started my journey in a lion cage
I was born in a river
I live in a jungle
I've got a furry coat
My friend is a gorilla
I swing from treetop to treetop
I kill dangerous animals
I eat leaves from trees

Abbas Nooh (7)
Deansfield Primary School

I'M A SPIDER IN THE GARDEN

I live in a drainpipe all by myself.
I started from my drainpipe.
I can go on a journey.
A fierce cat jumped out of the bushes and chased me.
I nearly broke my legs escaping from that cat.
Then I nearly got squashed by a glittering window on my
        exhausting day.
My dinner is a fly, yum.
After dinner I went back up my drainpipe.

Raif Karioglu (7)
Deansfield Primary School

MY JOURNEY TO SCHOOL

My backpack loaded and green ribbons in my hair,
It's so easy getting ready for school.
I'm ready for school,
I packed my pens and pencils,
Swimming costume and towel.
Mum said, 'Go to school.'
It's so easy getting ready for school,
I pack my stuff,
'Bye Mum.'
Off to school I go.

Hayleigh Spencer (8)
Deansfield Primary School

VOYAGE THROUGH THE BLUE

I am a fluffy bird on a long journey.
I have beautiful feathers and a long beak.
My name is Beauty because of my feathers.
I can see beautiful swans
Down below in the wavy water.
I have caught a fish for my family.
My voyage was brilliant.

Katherine Coogan (8)
Deansfield Primary School

MY JOURNEY BEGINS

My journey begins
In my mind.
I go forward
In time.
I could fly with no wings.
There are lots of lights.
I can run around Saturn's ring.

Charlie Amestoy (9)
Deansfield Primary School

I WOULD LOVE TO . . .

I would love to slide on Saturn's rings.
Run up the highest mountain.
Sunbathe on the sun.
Swim through space and dance on chocolate.

Charlotte Turner (10)
Deansfield Primary School

I AM A DIVER

I am a diver
I dive into the icy cold sea
I live and travel on a boat
I catch my colourful food
I nearly got eaten by a shark
I have been looking for a treasure chest full of gold and silver
My search was getting dangerous.

Charlie Hawker (8)
Deansfield Primary School

MY SPACE JOURNEY

I went into space
And saw an alien's face
His name was Fred
Fred was very nice
His second name was Price
On the way I saw big red Mars
It was as big as chocolate bars.

Millie Hurault (6)
Deansfield Primary School

MY MOST MAGICAL TRIP

I would love to fly on a glistening star.
I would love to run down the highest mountain.
I would love to swim in a baking volcano.
But most of all I would love to ski on the shining moon.

Hollie Parle (10)
Deansfield Primary School

JOSH THE BEAR MAN

Josh liked bears
He had 100 at least
From little bears to big hairy bears
An army of bears protected the house from any mouse
Bears were strong except the cubs
So they had a little club
They fought the dogs
They killed the cats
Josh trained his bears to do crafty tricks
They mugged a man and threw babies out of their prams
One night a burglar came in
The bears woke up and threw him in the bin

Josh O'Hara (10)
Gordonbrock Primary School

THE BEAST IN THE MIRROR

It stares at me whenever I glance
I find it hideous
Its spots bursting
Like a volcano about to erupt
The pointed nose sticking out
Like Cleopatra's Needle
Its eyes are a dull miserable shade of green
Like a stagnant pond
Its hair has a thousand knots
Like a spider's web
I want the mirror to crack
It stares at me whenever I glance.

Kasia Hastings (9)
Gordonbrock Primary School

THE WATERFALL

It's beautiful,
It's tropical,
It's a waterfall!
It runs through the night,
It runs in the afternoon
And gives some a fright.
Some think it's wonderful,
Some think it's a bore,
Some are just difficult
And others want more.
When the waves clash on the rocks
It's funny because it reminds me of pirates
Fighting and throwing glass on the top deck.
But there is a much softer, smooth and gentle drool
To a waterfall.

Jessie Rae Perkins (10)
Gordonbrock Primary School

MYSTERY MAMMAL

In she came from the cold outdoors,
Then like a ballerina she walked daintily across the floor,
Her pink paws and little nose, pink as candyfloss,
I could see her course straight for our pillows of moss,
She started to groom her long white hair,
Sitting comfortably on our velvet chair,
As she heard her owner call her name,
She ran as swift as a cheetah and came
Into the kitchen she went to devour her food,
That's my little white Persian cat, golden, good.

Rhiannon Warrener (10)
Gordonbrock Primary School

MY JOURNEY

I watch as the tracks whizz by
Like snakes slithering down a mountainy range.
I see cattle in the fields,
Standing, staring.
I watch raindrops trickling down my window.

I see fast-flowing rivers and emerald grass
And horses galloping past.
I watch, I see, the sun going down,
The sky changing colour,
Then, 'We will be arriving in Bournemouth in 20 minutes, thank you.'
I look even harder now and see, and see,
Stables and farmyards and far in the distance the sea, the sea!
Like a billowing, freshly-washed sheet hanging out on the washing line.

I arrive in the station safe and sound,
All in one piece as I step down to the ground.
I get into a taxi and think and think,
About all the great things I'm about to do.

Emine Yasemin Ali (10)
Gordonbrock Primary School

A TRAIN JOURNEY

I'm going on a train journey,
There's no knowing where I'm going.
I could be going to Scotland or Ireland,
But I hope I'm going to a place
Where there are giants and castles
And big hills like towering mountains.
I'm going on a train journey,
There's no knowing where I'm going.

Owen Plant (9)
Gordonbrock Primary School

THE THUNDERSTORM

The cliff face juts out like a broken bone jutting out of a body,
Grass sways in the wind,
The sea crashes against the rocks,
The flowers flutter prettily in the breeze,
Black rain clouds move overhead,
Rain starts trickling, pitter, patter, pitter, patter,

Suddenly *clash!* Rain falls down in torrents,
Lightning lights the sky and thunder booms,
The flowers are flattened to a pulp,
The grass stops swaying and the sea starts spraying water into the air,

Then the sun comes out and dries up the land,
The sea turns to its usual calm,
The grass still sways in the wind,
And a few flowers flutter in the breeze,
The cliff face still juts out as usual,
The beach is still the same.

Johannah Alltimes (9)
Gordonbrock Primary School

YOU ARE THE ONE

From all the rabbits in the world.
I have found you from yesterday!
I have walked around the world so long!
I am so tired.
I am so old.
But now I've found you from yesterday!
You are the one, you are the one.
My little rabbit, you are the one.

Gül Mulla (9)
Gordonbrock Primary School

THE VOLCANO

She explodes, as lava flies into the air,
Then like treacle it slithers fast or slow,
Silently like a snake or loud like a million car engines,
As it throws rock down, down onto a village.
As lava traps people in different shapes,
Looking like wax models covered in blood-red lava.
People run for their lives,
But they're too late,
As lava attacks them
Like an army of blood-red soldiers
Attacking with lava cannon balls.
Some people escape, others don't.
And now lava has covered the village.

Matthew Hauke (9)
Gordonbrock Primary School

I WANT!

I want a horse that is fat and coarse
I want a car that's speedy and fast
I want a PlayStation with all the latest games
I want a million shops, a ton of gel pens
I want a house with a thousand rooms
I want a zoo with one hundred baboons
I want a pet with its own training centre
I want a planet with its own alien shuttle
I want a beach paradise with a private swimming pool
I want a hi-fi with loads of CDs
I want a collection of make-up

I want, I want,
Don't get!

Clara Blow (10)
Gordonbrock Primary School

SUSIE

She prowls slowly along
Waiting for her prey to come slowly along
Her prey will be smelling of cheese

She squeezes through gaps in fences
And looks for her prey in long, wide fields
She calls for her friends to come and help

When her friends come and help
They go hunting for their dinner
And take it home to get praised

When she has been praised
She scoffs it down with happiness
And curls up for a long sleep

Judith Hamm (10)
Gordonbrock Primary School

SPIDER

This story you are about to hear
Will fill your heart with deadly fear
It takes place in a corridor
Where something lurks upon the floor
As deadly as a poisonous snake
As frightening as an earthquake
She sits and has to wait and wait
For a nice fly to take the bait
Then suddenly as quick as lightning
She pounces on the fly's wing
Wrapping it up like a cocoon
Saving it for the next full moon

Josie Fletcher-Bell (10)
Gordonbrock Primary School

CHEESE

Beady eyes and bony body
She sits in her cage
Watching everybody,

Sniffing nose and big front teeth,
She eats cheese and cats eat meat,

She runs around hiding from the cat,
Sometimes she hides under the mat,

She sits up straight when waiting for her cheese
Sitting in her bowl,

She looks around
But she had not found
Her cheese sitting in her bowl, her bowl,
Her cheese sitting in her bowl.

Ben Hauke (9)
Gordonbrock Primary School

THE GOLDEN DUNGEON

Golden dungeon you are so bright
You even glitter during the night
Your gold is nice
Even when you are frozen in ice
You seem to glitter like sparks sparkling bright.

I imagine the golden rides glittering in my head
You amaze me
You seem to be amazing although you are only gold.

Nereece Johnson (10)
Gordonbrock Primary School

WHEN YOU ARE LYING IN BED

When you are up and awake in the day,
you never know what to do or say.
But when you are lying down in bed,
you can read all sorts of stories to go into your head.
You can read about a brave knight going into war,
and you can read about a giant lion's roar.
You can read about a murderer on the run,
and you can read fiction books about Mother Teresa the nun.
You can read about witches, wizards and vampires too,
and you can read about a donkey with the name of Roo.
Then you can dream,
dream about the finest cream.

Hannah Redler (10)
Gordonbrock Primary School

MY DOG

My dog is a pain
He wrecks my garden
He bangs on the garden door until it will open
He comes in the house
Runs up and down
Jumps on the table
Jumps back down
Jumps on the sofa
Jumps back down
Jumps on my dad's shoulder
Like a talking parrot
When he hears the word 'dinner'
He goes crazy.

Ali Musa (9)
Gordonbrock Primary School

THE SNAKE

Covering the ground with her long body,
Waiting for her prey to come amongst her,
No need to be shy, she's very comforting,
    Her name is Lin.

Mothering her eggs with her cold skin,
Slithering down the rocks as fragile as a crystal,
Maybe she is scared of what I cannot think of.
    She is a *snake*.

Rosie Matilda Peters (9)
Gordonbrock Primary School

MY FISH

My fish has eyes as big as a small ball,
When it bubbles it means a call.
When it goes into the castle it gets stuck,
If it gets out it's my luck.
It looks like a black alien my fish,
So when I go by it always goes wissh.

Sujoy Mitra (9)
Gordonbrock Primary School

BLADE

There's an adorable puppy called Blade
Who went to Glades on his rollerblades
He went into Next
And bought a crossed stitch polo neck
And bladed home to his bed.

Mehmet Achik-El (10)
Gordonbrock Primary School

WHAT AM I?

Silent
Gigantic
Black
Invisible
Like a giant sink hole
Can only be seen by infra-red
It's dangerous near me
Be prepared to go at light speed
Can you guess what I am?
Do you need more clues?
Trying to get near me
My gravity's too dangerous
Like a bath with an open plug hole
Like a whirlpool in the sea
An upside-down tornado
Sucking up the clouds
Can't you still guess what I am?
Last chance!
Suck things up at light speed
You don't have a chance
Giving up already?
I pity you
I'll give you an answer
Your answer is
And always will be
A black hole
I'm silent
Gigantic
Black
Invisible

Dami Benbow (10)
Gordonbrock Primary School

My Fake Family

My brother is 16,
My sister is 4,
I am 14,
My mum is more.

My brother likes panthers,
My sister likes dogs,
I like horses,
My mum likes frogs.

My brother is an alien,
My sister is a freak,
I am normal,
My mum is weak.

My brother has a girlfriend,
My sister has a doll,
I have a computer,
My mum has a troll.

My brother eats cabbage,
My sister eats beans,
I eat sweetcorn,
My mum eats greens.

Helena Eastham (9)
Gordonbrock Primary School

The Sea

The sea, so calm, so cool
The sea, it felt likc a swimming pool!
But then I remembered that the sea is full of pollution and waste!
So I jumped out faster than anyone in the human race!

Isabel Mealey (8)
Muswell Hill Primary School

LIGHT AND DARK

One smells like strawberries, sugar and daffodils
The other smells like blood, death and smoke
One feels hot
The other feels cold
One is like summer
The other is like winter
One makes you feel free
Like a butterfly flying outside
The other makes you feel like you're trapped in a cave
With something in there waiting to eat you
One lives high above the sky
The other lives deep below the ground
One is shaped like a love heart
The other is shaped like a storm cloud
One moves wherever it wants to go
The other follows you wherever you go
Light and dark travel around the world holding hands
They keep each other company
They are connected to each other

Sarah Huckett (10)
Muswell Hill Primary School

THE PUMPKIN PATCH

In the pumpkin patch
Where the colours all match
There are lots of mice
That don't look nice.
There are also lots of rats
That are fun for the cats
That sleep on the mats
In the pumpkin patch.

Lee Shiouxios (9)
Muswell Hill Primary School

THE WEEKEND

The weekend is lovely,
No teachers!
No tests!
No work!

The weekend is lovely,
Go swimming,
Visit friends,
Eat out.

The weekend is boring,
Watch TV,
Do homework,
Stay in.

The weekend is boring,
Washing up,
Tidy my room,
Be good!

Alexandra Lambis (10)
Muswell Hill Primary School

SCHOOL

It's nine o'clock, school is on
It's time for work, I wish I was gone.
It's time for maths
It's such a long path
I wish I was in my lovely warm bath.
It's time for play, I feel gay
The time is ticking away
The bullies are going to throw away
What a lovely warm day.

Precious Omoregie (9)
Muswell Hill Primary School

A LITTLE SUN

My best thing about the weekend
Is you don't have to go to school.
It's so fun,
It's so wicked,
And it is so cool!
No more maths or history,
No more boring literacy.
No more school.
I like going to the rehearsals
For the show I'm in.
I like to challenge my mum to a game,
And see who will win.
I sleep in, in the mornings,
And stay up late at night.
The only thing I do not have is a pillow fight!
I like the weekends, they are so fun,
It's especially nice when there's a little sun!

Rebecca Mangin (10)
Muswell Hill Primary School

RABBITS

Rabbits, rabbits, they headbutt the cats.
They make a mat with human hats.
Rabbits, rabbis, they even make a cake
By a saucepan and bats.
Rabbits, rabbits they have habits.
Rabbits, rabbits they lost their habits.
Rabbits, rabbits they are dead from a fox forever.
Rabbits, rabbits they are no more.

Ashley Leigh (9)
Muswell Hill Primary School

THE BOLD EAGLE

He swoops around for human prey
And glares about for juicy stuff
He listens intensely, hears a bray
The, he shoots down and attacks
The beast and gains a cut
To fair out the deal!
Wind flying past him, the animal in his beak
Flies past a mountain, nice and sleek
He pays no attention to the passers-by
No one will try to make this bird die!
The baby awaits with an appetite
Shrieking and squeaking for a bite
No one knows, everyone cares
How the bold eagle does for his dares!
He starts to glide again, azure all around him
Being unnoticed by the birds of prey
No one wants to
No one can kill *all* the bold eagles of the hills!

Amos Schonfield (8)
Muswell Hill Primary School

STICKY TOFFEE

I'm hot and happy,
I'm running very fast.
I hope I will,
But I might not last.
We're playing sticky toffee,
And we're wasting our play,
Because it's not a very good game,
To play on a hot day.

Chloe Kraemer (7)
Muswell Hill Primary School

THE WEEKEND

It's Friday and the week is done,
It's time to relax and have some fun.
I slump on the sofa to watch TV,
All I want to watch is channel 3.
I ask for a snack, then ask again,
My brother will tease me while playing a game.
It's time for a bath before bed,
My brother's a real sleepy head.
The next day I shop with my mum,
And beg her for money to get me some gum.
The rest of the day is the same as before,
Until a letter falls onto the floor.
It's from my cousin Becky,
Who I think is really quite pretty.
She's asking me over for a week and a day,
I give a great shout of *'Hooray!'*
My mum says, 'Yes, of course we can go.'
I hear my brother give a great sigh of, 'Doh!'
It's Sunday night, washing my hair,
Oh how I wish my hair was fair!
I'm getting my homework ready for school,
And my brother is still playing the fool!

Sophie Volhard (10)
Muswell Hill Primary School

SUNDAY

You know the next day's gonna be school and that's not any fun,
So go and have a dip in the pool and buy a cream bun.
If that does not cheer you up, go to a pet shop and buy a little pup,
But if that surprise plan does fail, go to the zoo to see the whales,
And if you're still out of luck, you know the next day's gonna suck.

Jesse Dangoor (11)
Muswell Hill Primary School

WILD HORSES

Galloping through the wild wide forest
Looking for someone to play
To jump and leap in a big pile of hay.
As he runs wild and free
All the green things he can see.
The things that he likes to eat
Is much better than a lump of meat.
Then he smiles in delight
When he sees something white
It's a white female horse.
So he dances in delight
Of finding his friend at last.
The two horses trotting and galloping in the forest
Find a load of camping tourists.
They run away in fright
Because they would have to stay the night
In a cage.
In the morning at sunrise
They run off to the golden sun.

Beth Willow Hurst Lawley (9)
Muswell Hill Primary School

SUNDAY

S   unday, I haven't done my homework
U   nder my bed it is laying there
N   ow it is time to eat my Sunday roast
D   ownstairs I watch TV
A   nd still have to do my homework
Y   awning and groaning I go upstairs and do my homework
     Tomorrow is Monday, I have to go to school

Rachel Stanigar (10)
Muswell Hill Primary School

LIGHT AND DARK

Two separate forces that blend together
Light brings happiness
Dark brings sadness
Light is a lion
It feels like velvet
The colour of creamy yellow
It looks like children in a playground playing
It smells like cool juicy ice lollies
Dark is a dragon
It feels smooth but bumpy
Black and mauve are dark's colours
It looks like a graveyard, silent and empty
It smells like plum pudding, sweet and sour
Light lives in the sun
Dark lives in the moon
Light moves at the speed of sound
Dark moves at the speed of light
No matter how hard you try
Light and dark cannot be separated.

Liam Caulfield (9)
Muswell Hill Primary School

WEEKEND AT THE CIRCUS

W e went to the circus at the weekend
E very hair on our heads were standing on end
E ach skilful movement was graceful and neat
K eeping us glued to the edge of our seat
E xciting it was for each one in the ring
N o one could bear to be missing a thing
D isappointment now. It's over.

Leo Fordham (11)
Muswell Hill Primary School

LIGHT AND DARK

Two separate forces that blend together
Light brings happiness
Dark brings sadness.

Light is a leopard
It feels like soft fur
It is a shiny gold colour
It smells like a flower
It looks like chocolate that makes your mouth water
It lives on the sun.

Dark is a dragon
It feels like a slimy slug
It is a dark black colour
It smells like rotten eggs
It looks like a black hole
It lives on the moon.

Light and dark need each other
To help make the world a better place.

Jake Moxon (10)
Muswell Hill Primary School

LIGHT AND DARK

The sun, a ball of fire that shines on the Earth,
Dark is cool and a shiver that no one can describe,
Light is refreshing, warm and bright
Dark is dry and mouldy,
Light lives in your heart that brightens up your body,
Light smells like a flower,
Dark lives in the world waiting to explode,
Dark smells like acid.

Dwight Leiba-Rennie (10)
Muswell Hill Primary School

THE RABBIT

The rabbit hops from side to side
He puffs his chest out with pride
He hops and hops all day long
Until he hears the gong

The rabbit goes to bed
Instead of having all the fun
And after that he wants to eat
A nice hot currant bun

Why does he go to sleep
Instead of his mother reading Bo Peep?
If he does not go to school
He won't be cool at all

Little rabbits go to school every day
Rabbit doesn't just sit, he plays
And when it's time for bed he sits
And listens to the insects like crickets.

Rachel Sandler (9)
Muswell Hill Primary School

LIGHT AND DARK

Light is jumping up on Christmas morning.
Dark feels cold and miserable.
Dark is war.
Light is world peace.
Dark feels hatred in your heart.
Light feels love blossoming in your heart.

Light bright.
Dark shark.

Akash Singh (10)
Muswell Hill Primary School

LIGHT AND DARK

Light is a lion, it roars its way around,
Dark is a dragon with ferocious fiery breath,
Light is the daytime,
Dark is the night,
Light and dark need each other,
To survive.

Light feels weightless,
Soft and silky,
Light smells like honey,
Sweet and thick,
Light looks like buttercups,
And a field full of cows,
Light tastes like ice lollies,
Cool and juicy.

Dark feels heavy,
Cold and bumpy,
Dark smells like rubbish,
Old and mouldy,
Dark looks like thunder clouds,
Ready to burst,
Dark tastes like ash,
Burnt and dusty.

Light is an apple pie,
Dark is a plum pudding,
Without each other dark and light would . . .
   Die!

Elizabeth Donker Curtius (10)
Muswell Hill Primary School

LIGHT AND DARK

Light

Light is a friendship,
Circled with daises.

Light is happiness and smiles,
A sun glistening at dawn.

Light is a bright sky,
Sparkling stars at night.

Light is magical,
A feeling that never leaves.

Light is a burning fire,
A happy face.

Dark

Dark is an argument,
Ugly and mean.

Dark is a piercing eagle's call,
A pitch-black sky.

Dark is an evil feeling,
Which hurts inside.

Dark is sad,
Unkind.

Dark is mysterious,
And it scares you.

Lois Bond (10)
Muswell Hill Primary School

LIGHT AND DARK

Two separate forces that blend together
Loneliness and popularity have big differences
Death and life, what enemies they were
Light feels like a soft rose
Light looks like soft autumn leaves
The colour of light is a rich yellow
Light has many different shapes
Light is a fast moving rabbit
Light is the smell of a sweet daffodil
It lives everywhere
It lives because it is magical
It flies around
It survives by flying away from the dark

Dark is gooey
It looks like an old pig
It's a mouldy green and purple
Dark is a shape with no name
Dark is a slow old black elephant
Dark lives in a dark smelly grave
Dark lives by chasing light
It moves by slipping up and down
It survives by letting dark go

Nicholas Lee Kerle (9)
Muswell Hill Primary School

DINOSAURS

I'm interested in dinosaurs,
They scratch others with their claws.
Wow, they're big,
But they're thick,
And they've got big jaws.

They run in big packs,
But they can't scratch their backs.
Some are pretty,
Some are witty,
And some fall in the sack.

Stefan Phillips (9)
Muswell Hill Primary School

LIGHT AND DARK

Two separate forces that blend together,
Light and dark make the world,
Light and dark, how different they are,
Light feels like a breeze of wind,
Light looks like a white dove,
Light is any colour it wants to be,
Light is any shape it wants to be,
Light is a fast, ferocious squirrel,
Light smells like freshly-cut grass,
Light lives on the clouds,
Light lives by feeding off the sun's rays,
Light survives by moving at the speed of light away from its predators.
Dark feels like mouldy leaves,
Dark looks like a black, decaying mountain goat,
Dark is dark green,
Dark's shapes are anything it wants to be,

Dark is a plant-eating devil,
Dark smells like horse manure,
Dark lives in a smouldering volcano,
Dark lives by feeding off darkness,
Dark moves at the speed of light,
Dark survives by chasing light around the world.

Joe Bourne (9)
Muswell Hill Primary School

LIGHT AND DARK

Two separate forces that blend together
They're like the pen and pen-lid needing each other,
They're battling but they are still *one* army.

Light feels like the calming breeze of fresh air,
The bright colours fill your brain,
Light comes in all shapes and sizes,
Light lives at the heart of the sun,
Aliens are the creatures of light,
Light is the fastest thing on earth.

Dark is the eye of the storm,
There's bright colours but dark colours,
Dark is patterns, dark is splodges, dark is patches, dark is splashes,
Dark's creature is a black adder,
Dark smells like black pudding,
Dark creeps towards you and suddenly it *springs.*
The light and the dark's survival kits are each other.

Hannah E M Hughes (10)
Muswell Hill Primary School

MY MUM

My mum is cool and tall
And she is kind and doesn't mind
When I climb up the wall

She lets me annoy her when I'm cheeky
She doesn't mind
That's why my mum is so kind

Tom Shaer (9)
Muswell Hill Primary School

LIGHT AND DARK

You are light when you have an A+.
You are dark when you have an F-.
You are light when you are going on holiday.
You are dark when you're bored at home.
You are light when you have a baby brother.
You are dark when someone dies.

You are light when you're in the sunshine.
You are dark when it is raining.

You are light when you are happy.
You are dark when you are sad.
You are light when school ends.
You are dark when school starts.
You are light when you get a pet.
You are dark when your pet dies.

You feel light when you meet a new teacher.
You feel dark when you leave a teacher.

Max Edward Rossiter (9)
Muswell Hill Primary School

MY PET MOUSE

My pet mouse has a very big house
It doesn't like cheese
And it has very small knees
And it really hates bees.

Some pet mice don't like woodlice
Especially my mouse
That lives in a big house.

Oscar Downey (9)
Muswell Hill Primary School

THE CRUELLEST WEEKENDS

You think the weekends are the best.
You look forward to the weekend
And when you get there you think you've passed the test!
But you haven't, you've got homework,
Your parents ask you to do chores.
But wait, that's just the beginning, there's even more!
Rainy days, work, cleaning, no break,
Just work, and moan to bits!
But *my* weekends are horrible,
I argue, do homework, clean
And I always end up in missy fits!

You just have to try and find one good thing, just one.
But all I can think of is *none!*
Some of you may have good weekends,
But think of us who don't!
We are forced to do things that we don't want to do,
But there is no chance of saying won't!

So here I come to an impeccably lovely end!
Because I have to do horrible things for the worst weekend!

Kristina Goggin (11)
Muswell Hill Primary School

LIGHT AND DARK

The world was in darkness, there was no sun so nothing could grow.
The world was lonely and desolate but worst of all no stars.
The villagers complained to the creatures and they were furious.
They exploded and made the stars and the big boss was so, so, so angry
He made the biggest explosion of all
And that made the sun, so that is how the stars came into the world.

Thomas Winnington (9)
Muswell Hill Primary School

THE DOLPHIN

I stand on a rock, watching the sea
Suddenly I see the swish of a tail
The dolphin skimming through the waves
He looks so pale.

I rush down the rocks
Just in time,
I plunge into the waters
To hear a whine.

I spy the dolphin,
The water's so cool,
He flaps away the fish in a school.

I hold his fin
We skim away
Into the deep blue waters
But I don't know which way.

But who cares? Not me or the dolphin.

Emma Fleur Magnus (9)
Muswell Hill Primary School

I WANT TO BE A PILOT

I want to be a pilot and swoop in the sky.
I want to glide beside the mountain tops or just fly high.
When I glide by the mountain tops
Down below I hear the clanging of pots.
I fly with the birds before half-past seven
But I've got to be careful not to follow them to Devon.
That will be my dream come true
But first I've got to tell it to you.

Giannini Chambers (9)
Muswell Hill Primary School

THE WONDERS OF THE WORLD

The ice is cold where the penguins live
But their feathers keep them warm.
They splash in the sea
And have fish for tea
And they can come to no harm.

The land is hot where the volcano is
And when lava starts to rise
The people scream, shout,
Run about
And cry and dry their eyes.

It is windy where the tornado is
And people get lifted in the air.
Everyone's nightmare
Is this frightener
And this is everyone's scare.

So now you know that people here
Are always scared and bold
And I have told you
In this poem
The wonders of the world.

Madeleine Wickers (9)
Muswell Hill Primary School

LIGHT AND DARK

Light

Light is a special star in the sky.
Light is warm on a cold winter's night.
Light is like the clearest crystal pool.

Dark

Dark is like a mysterious shadow.
Dark is frightening and fun.
Dark is a shadow that covers the sun.

Yoni Pakleppa (9)
Muswell Hill Primary School

THE ROCKET

The rocket blasts off at the speed of light
It looks like a shiny meteorite.
We're going to Mars
To look at the stars.
We've been to the moon
But came back too soon.

The captain is called Jake
And he has a pet snake.
He has been to lots of stars
But he has never been to Mars.
The navigator's skill is so bad
We don't know if we'll get there,
He's totally mad.

We landed on Mars with a great big crash
There was a dent in the rocket because of the smash.
'Will we get home?' the crew all cried.
'I think so,' the captain replied.
They blasted off at the speed of light again.
Will they reach Earth? Who knows?
The end.

Felix Volhard (7)
Muswell Hill Primary School

SEASONS

The year starts with spring,
In spring the bluebells bloom
And the world has made a fling.
The calves are born,
The farmers plant their corn
And that is our friend called
    Spring!

After spring comes summer
And the sun starts on a runner.
We all eat ice cream
And nobody's mean.
That is our friend called
    Summer!

Autumn comes next
And the trees all shed
And through the muddy fields watered.
That is our friend called
    Autumn!

Next winter is here
And grown-ups drink lots of beer
With frostbite outside.
Christmas is on our side.
When Christmas comes we're all merry.
Grown-ups drink small glasses of sherry.

So now you know how the seasons change.

Mirella Wilson (9)
Muswell Hill Primary School

THE WILD TIGER

The tiger runs so swift
for it has a gift
of legs that run so fast
that it couldn't be last
in an animal race
with its incredible pace

The tiger has all types
of different kinds of stripes
and it has no fear
It can sense if something's near
and it is very rare
it's faster than a hare

The tiger is so calm
it ate out of my palm
and even though it eats
horrible types of meats
let me give you some advice
tigers are very nice

The tiger stares at me
as peaceful as can be
and as you can see
I'm kneeling on my knee
crouching in the dark
the tiger's eyes make a spark

Amber Tipper (8)
Muswell Hill Primary School

THE DRAGON AND THE BEAR

The dragon is burning down all the houses
Days do come, years do passes.

Then finally their hope is there
A gigantic black and white bear.
Hey, is something wrong here?
But the villagers did not care.

The only thing that bear did do
Was eat some honey and make a foe.

But that foe was the mighty dragon.
So one day the dragon flew away.
So the villagers and the bear could stay.

Saul Goldblatt (10)
Muswell Hill Primary School

THE BUFFALO

Faster than wind he charges
As he runs his back arches

He spins around and around
As his front hooves paw the ground

He spins, he charges around
Without a single sound

He dances
He prances

In the cool shade
Of a green, green glade.

Abbey Garrood (8)
Muswell Hill Primary School

SUNDAY NIGHT

S ometimes I haven't done my homework!
U nder and over I can't find it anywhere.
N orth and south, east and west.
D ragging on and on the day goes by.
A nd at last I find it.
Y awning and groaning I struggle through it.

N ow I have finished, I start to get comfy.
I hear my mum calling:
'G eorgia it's time for tea!
H urrying my tea until it's
T V time, I stay up late staring blankly.

Georgia Lansdown (10)
Muswell Hill Primary School

SUNDAY NIGHT

S mell of roast chicken fills the air.
U p early tomorrow, back to school.
N auseous sprouts on the table.
D elicious spuds on my plate.
A lexandra Palace ice rink is where I'm going.
Y ellow lights glisten in the dark.

N ight-time comes, I go to bed.
I   brush my teeth, it's getting late.
G oing to bed, setting my alarm.
H aving trouble resting my eyes.
T omorrow morning I despise.

Jamie Adams (10)
Muswell Hill Primary School

THE VICTORIANS

T he name of the Queen's husband was Albert
H e died from an illness that was caused by water
E ven the rich boys would wear dresses

V ictoria was a very famous queen, do you know why?
I t was 1800 that this queen did reign
C old winters are very bad for the homeless
T ill 1901 was the full reign of this famous queen
O h so much they did for us
R unning electricity for better light
I t was not too good for the children
A t last a man stopped this which is good for me
N ow we've made it better
S o there you have it, what else can I say?

Ayesha Chinn (10)
Muswell Hill Primary School

SUNDAY NIGHT

S unday nights are very fun
U nder the heat of the fire we sit
N onchalantly watching football
D ad is pleased with our score right now
A nd sits there waiting for a goal
Y et I am playing with my hamster

N ot aware of the score
I t's a goal!
'G reat one!' screams Dad
'H old it,' says Mum
'T ime for bed.' *Boo!*

James Simpson (11)
Muswell Hill Primary School

LIGHT AND DARK

L ight is a candle, the sun, a torch,
I ndigo, green, orange, yellow, red, blue and violet makes white light,
G reen, blue and red are primary colours,
H eat is made by the sun,
T orches flash and make lots of light,

A nything can absorb light,
N o light can go through opaque objects,
D on't look straight at the sun,

D arkness is made when the sun goes down,
A nd nocturnal creatures come out,
R ainbows are made when it's raining but sunny,
K ids don't like the dark.

Martha Young (10)
Muswell Hill Primary School

LIGHT AND DARK

L ight is very bright
I like light, it makes you feel happy
G oing to your friends makes you very happy
H olidays make you feel bright and happy
T winkling stars are very light

A nd so is the moon
N obody's light on rainy days
D etention is very dark

D ark is very sad and dull
A nything could be light or dark
R ed can be very dark
K illing is very dark.

Oliver De Wan (10)
Muswell Hill Primary School

THE SNAKE

He comes slithering up and down
Mostly touching the ground
Keep well hidden
He'll be forbidden
From slithering up and down.

He slithers at day
No time for play
That squiggly, squarmy snake.

Landrake is his name
He's definitely quite plain
And no time for a game
That squiggly, squarmy Landrake the snake
So terribly fake
The Landrake snake is . . .
Fake!

Imogen Rance (9)
Muswell Hill Primary School

A LOVELY NAN

My nan is a lovely woman
She cuddles me at night
And even though she cares for me
She keeps me up all night.

My nan buys me an iced bun
And I eat it like bubblegum
Yum-yum in my tum-tum.

Though my nan died in October
I'd really, really like to hold her.

Georgia Anderson (8)
Muswell Hill Primary School

SATURDAY

I wake and look at the clock.
O yes it's Saturday morning.
I turn and ignore that clock.
I try to dream of Robbie Williams.

Sleep does not come my way.
It's now 10:00am.
I jump out of bed.
I get ready for the wonderful day ahead.
My friend is coming over.
She is going to stay overnight.
That is what I like about Saturday.
Your friends can stay at night, on Saturday night.
I get excited.
Oops!
On the last step I trip over.
We laugh together
And leave for the wonderful day ahead.

Ziggy Hasan (10)
Muswell Hill Primary School

DARK AND LIGHT

Two separate forces that blend together.
Mix to make the world free.
Light sounds like a cockerel crowing in the morning.
Light smells like a meadow on a hot summer's day.
Dark is calm.
Dark is like an owl hooting in the night.
Dark smells like fear.
Dark feels like a bottomless pit.
Dark sounds like a wolf howling at the moon.

Tom Hatherley (10)
Muswell Hill Primary School

LIGHT AND DARK

Two separate forces that blend together
The happiness and sadness of the world
That makes night and day exist
Light sounds like a lion roaring
Light makes you feel safe and secure
Smells like a sunflower in a meadow
Looks like a cornfield swaying in the wind,
Dark makes you fell like you are in a lonely cave
Dark is like a sly fox seeing its innocent prey
Dark smells like dust and filth
Dark is grey and black
Light and dark could not survive without each other
Dark lives with devils in the underworld
And light is a god itself
Light travels gracefully and calmly
Dark goes through every soul in the world
Light and dark feed on each other.

Sean Wilkinson (9)
Muswell Hill Primary School

DARK AND LIGHT

Two separate forces blend together,
Light is the bride and dark is the groom,
Light smells like fresh golden hair,
Dark lives under your bed,
Dark and light form as one in perfect harmony,
Dark is cunning, clever and slow
It senses danger approaching,
Light is shy, happy and merry,
Light is the biggest day of your life

Aimee MacKenzie (9)
Muswell Hill Primary School

Sunny And Milky

They both lie on the grass
As the sun goes past
Then they get up arm in arm
And they walk so very calm
As they say goodbye their fur rubs against each other
And they go inside to their mother
As Milky goes down the path so quite alone
Thinking dreamily of his home
She begins to cry as he stops in some gum
But amazingly here comes her mum
Then they go inside
And Milky goes to hide
She is found and goes to have a bath
And there is no longer anybody walking down the path.

Hannah Johnson (9)
Muswell Hill Primary School

Sunday Night

Sunday is sour
Sunday is tight
I would much rather be in a bad fight
My mother says with a great might,
'You should not go out and fight.'
When it is night
I have a big fright
For the monsters under my bed
On Sunday night
I squeeze up tight
To my soft toy Spike
He will protect me from what I fear on Sunday night.

Matthew McLoughlin (10)
Muswell Hill Primary School

LIGHT AND DARK

Light and dark feed on each other
They are friends and enemies in different ways
They combine their powers to make day and night

Light spreads happiness to all faces
Light is like a kitten springing after a cotton ball
Light makes you feel fresh and clean
Without light the world would be nothing

Dark looks empty and bewildered
Dark sounds like an animal in sorrow
Dark feels soft and silky
Dark is like a big black cover protecting us

Dark and light are two forces that are so strong they can never
be broken

Light and dark must meet somewhere - but where?

Imogen Buxton (9)
Muswell Hill Primary School

MY SUNDAY

It's Sunday and tomorrow is Monday
And I still haven't done my homework.
And if I don't do my homework
I will be in at playtime.
It's ten o'clock at night
And I still don't know what to do.
Shall I give it in
Or shall I just relax and eat my roast dinner?
Or shall I just go to sleep
And forget about it?

Nima Toserkani (11)
Muswell Hill Primary School

LIGHT AND DARK

Two separate forces that blend together
Light and dark forces alliance
Light and dark can be put together like a jigsaw puzzle

Light smells like lemon zest
Dark smells like mouldy eggs, stuffy and cramped
Light feels like ear plugs and cotton
Dark feels wrinkled and hard as rock
Light is the colour of fiery red, burning orange and yellow
Dark is the colour of mouldy black and icky grey

Light is the goldenest sound of all sounds
Dark is the sound of crashing thunder, crackling lightning
Light lives in a tiger's lair
Dark lives in a castle of stone.

Thomas Glover
Muswell Hill Primary School

SUNDAY NIGHT

S   unday night, the last of the week,
U   nbelievably hectic,
N   ow let me see,
D   id I remember to pack up my bag?
A   m I seriously about to go mad?
Y   ou really don't know, how hard it can be.

N   ow did I remember to see
I   f I put my pencil case away?
G   oodness, Sunday nights are such a pain!
H   onestly, I truly declare,
T   onight is the night I get quite a scare.

Lottie Guy (11)
Muswell Hill Primary School

LIGHT AND DARK

Two separate forces that blend together,
Light a burning shine,
Dark a shadow in the light,
the two together make day and night.

The sun is the most important source of light,
as it burns it gives us light,
light is a colour nobody can describe,
light lives in your garden so you can play in it.

Dark, a lonely land,
that nobody wants to be in,
dark is loud but you can't hear it,
dark lives under your bed waiting to scare you.

Emerald A Robertson-Rose (9)
Muswell Hill Primary School

I WANT TO BE A FOOTBALLER

I want to be a footballer
And always have things my way.
I want to be a footballer
And get paid millions of pounds every day.

I'd buy all the best players
And a goalie who can catch,
And our team would be the best
And we'd win every match.

After we've beaten all the English teams
We'll travel overseas.
And we'll show all the foreign teams
We're the best that we can be!

Nathan Travers (9)
Muswell Hill Primary School

LIGHT AND DARK

Light and dark are the most powerful things in the universe.
They have advantages and disadvantages,
They are objects that we will never know the truth about.

Dark is cold and damp.
Dark spreads an empty feeling around us.
Dark makes us feel like we are dying down.

Light is a new beginning.
Light weaves its way round the world.
Light scares away the dark corners.

Dark and light deny each other.
Dark and light are like two eyes watching over us.

Clara Baldock (10)
Muswell Hill Primary School

BOOKS

Books are all different shapes and sizes,
Books that are dull and books that win prizes.
Books from England, books from Spain,
Some books even have the same name.

Some books are adventurous,
Some books are sad,
And some books are very, very bad.

Some books are romantic,
Some books are scary,
And some books are about a little duck called Mary.

Books are the best, as good as they can be,
Books stretch as far as the eye can see.

Caitlin Boswell-Jones (9)
Muswell Hill Primary School

SUNDAY NIGHT

On Sunday night I feel lazy and tired.
I don't want to go back to school.
I feel depressed and sad,
There's no interesting television on.
Sunday night is deep crimson.
Sunday night is the sound of silence.
Eight o'clock Monday means early to bed.
The weekends late nights means sleep doesn't come.
Millennia pass as I lie awake.
But still Monday morning comes too soon.
Sunday night fills me with dread because on Monday morning
I'll have to get out of bed.

Louis Marsh (11)
Muswell Hill Primary School

BEST WEEKEND

I wake up in the morning.
I play on Pokémon silver.
Down the stairs to watch TV.
My sister comes to watch with me.
We have breakfast
Then we get ready for Grandma's house,
And arrive in time for lunch.
More TV.
At five o'clock it's time for tea.
We always play for the rest of the day.
At seven we leave Grandma's house.
Home we go.
We want to go to sleep.

Ben Gilbert (10)
Muswell Hill Primary School

COLOURS OF THE RAINBOW

Red is a beautiful, blooming rose
And when I smell it, it tickles my nose.
Yellow is the shining sun
And while it's pretty I like to have lots of fun.
Purple is a lovely, juicy plum
And I love to eat it right into my tum.
Blue is a pretty, brilliant sea
I like to watch it while eating my tea.
Orange is a fire burning in the darkness
And every second it gets higher and higher.
Pink is the glistening paint on the wall
Even though it's quite bright it's also quite faint.

Alexandra Karavias (8)
Muswell Hill Primary School

GIRLS FOOTBALL DAY

Just after school, when the bell goes
A long wide smile on my face grows.
I slip in my boots and grab a ball,
Then outside I hear my friends call.
We ran down the road and onto the park
And set up the pitch to play before dark.
I went into the centre then the whistle blew,
I got the ball and just flew.
Nobody can get the ball off me.
I kicked the ball and it went into the back of the net.
I jumped up and down and screamed out loud
Inside me I felt strong and proud.

Rachel Weekes (9)
Muswell Hill Primary School

A GOLDEN GAZE

A golden gaze on a lion's face
He jumps and leaps at his own pace.
Lions like a piece of meat
Just a little something to eat.

He sees a zebra and leaps
And gets meat in heaps and heaps.
Then all he does is eat and eat
And that's a load of meat.

After that he lies and growls
A bit like a wolf howls.
Then he falls fast asleep
And does not make a single peep.

Jessica Louise Pitts Brennan (9)
Muswell Hill Primary School

SUNDAY NIGHT

S   mells of roast dinner
U   tterly nice
N   oise of clattering pots and pans
D   rowns out thoughts of school
A   ll through the meal
Y   ou dread what the next day will bring

N   ow the weekend ends
I   hope to see my friends
G   et my homework ready
H   appily watch TV
T   omorrow drifts away from me.

Michael Simpson (10)
Muswell Hill Primary School

ANIMALS

Animals, animals, they're the best
But sometimes they are a bit of a pest
Animals, animals are something mad
Even when they're being bad

Animals, animals have lots of fun
Especially when they lie under the sun
Animals, animals eat food a lot
But never ever make a plot

Animals, animals never have a bet
So that means they are good pets
Animals, animals aren't a door
But sometimes lie on the floor

Animals, animals are sometimes green
Even though they're not mean
Animals, animals are never late
I think animals are great!

Saskia Harrison (8)
Muswell Hill Primary School

LIGHT AND DARK

Light is like a wind of air
Dark feels like a damp sewer
Light is like a multicoloured rainbow
Dark smells like a stream of burning lava
Light moves as a gust of wind and lives in that air
Dark moves like the slowest creature
Dark lives in the darkest shadow
Light is the shape of the widest ocean

Chinua Phinn-Archer (10)
Muswell Hill Primary School

MY WEEKEND

My weekend's never very bad.
It's sometimes really fun,
But now you're asking me,
What the worst thing about my weekend seems to be,
It's certainly . . .
That I'm constantly . . .
Surrounded by my family!
My brothers wake up screaming,
(I think I should still be dreaming)
At 7 o'clock in the morning,
So I spend the whole day yawning.
My parents are always on at me,
For reasons which I fail to see.
The rabbits still need cleaning out,
The hamster's next without a doubt.
I s'pose it's better than being at school,
But the amount of homework's really cruel!
By the time I've finally got it done,
I'm back at school,
Where's all the fun?
I've got choir on Sunday afternoons,
My brothers are still acting like baboons,
I've gotta get my violin out 'n' play some tunes!
Why am I surrounded by all these loons?

Alice Clara Engelhard (11)
Muswell Hill Junior School

THE WORST THING ABOUT MY WEEKEND

The worst thing about my weekend has to be,
We can't do the things we want to do.
'Clean out the hamster.'
'I'll give you one back if you do the washing up.'
'Do your homework.'
'Gina, I need to speak to you.'
'Georgina come and see what I've done on the computer.'
'You're allowed chocolate if you do your homework.'
Things like that make me go off in a huff.
But that is after I stand there in a daze,
Just before I come back to my senses.
The homework lies forgotten.
It's in my bag at the bottom.
'Georgina there's dessert on the table.'
'Georginnaaaaa do your homework!'
'What!' I shout back up the stairs.
'Do your . . .'
The rest got drowned by a horrible noise.
Oh no, Hannah is playing her clarinet.
Do I stand here in a daze?
Yes I do.
Before I get back my senses.
I need the loo
But I've got so much to do.
Do I stand here in a daze?

Georgina Gainsley (10)
Muswell Hill Primary School

BEING IN LIGHT, BEING IN DARK

There's a rumour going round,
Other people know, everyone except me,
Why can't I know?
I've asked everybody - Janice, Tom and Lulu,
They're in the light, how come?
Why does everybody stare at me and point?
It's Jack Brigs isn't it?
He's always spreading rumours, especially about me.

I'm in the dark.

Niamh Mealey (9)
Muswell Hill Primary School

SUNDAY

S   mells of roast chicken fill the air,
U   nderwear and mess everywhere,
N   aughty kids playing in the park,
D   ares being made in the dark,
A   lways happy and well fed,
Y   awning, crawling up to bed!

Annabel Miles (11)
Muswell Hill Primary School

THE SONG OF THE SEA

I hear the sea rumbling
I hear the waves tumbling

I hear the wind whistling past my ear
I hear the sirens singing as they come near

They bring dark mist that covers the sea
I close my eyes and they are part of me

They take me back into the sea again
I open my eyes and I am one of them.

Gabriella Lewis (8)
Muswell Hill Primary School

THE WEEKEND

It's half-past three,
The children shout with glee.
As the children get their coats and bags,
As they run home thinking, 'Two days without any work.'
Not knowing what lurks inside the bags.
A page or two of homework there
To try and stop the fun.
When Monday comes around
It is still not done.

Stephanie Laredo (11)
Muswell Hill Primary School

RAIN

Water, water, water, rain, rain, rain,
Every weekend is the same,
Each drop that is falling is making it more appalling.
Keeps raining, it keep pouring, every weekend is boring.
Exciting? No way! It's even more boring than hay!
Nobody could stop it even with a mop.
Distant voices are calling, rain is appalling.

Raul Balchin-Qais (11)
Muswell Hill Primary School

THE BEST THING ABOUT THE WEEKEND!

I went to a party on Saturday night,
I didn't know what to wear,
But I thought I might
Wear my shoes that are far too tight.

I wish the weekend would never end,
With lots of fun and laughter,
Where I do great things,
Like ride my bike,
And play with the friends I like.

Ffion Knaggs (11)
Muswell Hill Primary School

SUNDAY

S   ee my homework not done
U   nlearned spellings on the floor
N   ine times tables lay forgotten
D   irty PE kit in the basket
A   red maths sheet under the bed
Y   esterday's cinema tickets in the bin.

Eleanor Morgan (11)
Muswell Hill Primary School

LIGHT AND DARK

Light is very bright.
It is a dazzling sight.
Glittering and glinting.
Hundreds of shining lights.
The sun is a blazing ball of light.

Dark is damp.
A gloomy dull sight.
Rough and cold.
Killing is dark and horrible.

Claire Cadman (9)
Muswell Hill Primary School

LIGHT AND DARK

Light is very fast,
It travels in straight waves.
Goodness is light,
Happiness comes, sadness goes,
Temperature changes with light around.

Dark is evil,
A cave is dark,
Remaining evil and unshining,
Kills the light out of sight.

Adam Rosenfeld (9)
Muswell Hill Primary School

I AM MAD

I am absolutely mad.
I'm happy, I never get sad.
But then it's time for bed
I cannot rest my head
So I just stay up
Till twelve instead.

Grace Hill (9)
Muswell Hill Primary School

MY BEST FRIEND

My best friend is really nice
But she is not scared of mice.
She's really fun
And she's got a really sweet bunny.

She's really cool
And she's not a fool.
Me and my best friend
Jumped in the swimming pool.
She's got brown hair
And in PE we were in a pair.

We've both got the same pencil cases
And I help her with her shoe laces.
When I'm in the way of something
She really doesn't mind.

Aneesa Mushtaq (9)
Muswell Hill Primary School

THE BLIND DOG

I guide my friend
Round every bend
I see without
A thought for me.
Whenever I see danger
I yelp to help you see.
I bark if I see a lark fluttering round my master's head
As I lead him home to bed.

Lewis Buxton (7)
Muswell Hill Primary School

FOOTBALL

I got the ball
I dodged, I swerved
I kicked it hard
And saw it curve
Oh no! It hit the post
I was mad
And at the end of the game
My team was really sad

The next match I played
It rained so hard. It was delayed
I told the ref to hurry up
He said the lights had broken down
So we had to play the match at Kentish Town.

Thomas Engelhard (8)
Muswell Hill Primary School

THAT'S MINE

That's my teddy,
Because it's got a ribbon saying Neddy.
That's my hook,
Because it says my name Brook.

That's mine, that's mine!

That's my dolly,
Because its name is Polly.
That's my dog,
Because he has a toy log.

That's mine, that's mine!
All mine!

Lisa Cannon (8)
Sacred Heart RC Primary School

I Can't Think

I can't think
My pen has no ink
My paper is blank
My learning has sank

I can't think
I need a drink
I have a broken seat
I need my wheat

I can't think
School is the weakest link
My life's gone down the sink
I think I'm on the brink . . . of a nervous breakdown

Alex Stoakes (9)
Sacred Heart RC Primary School

Going To The Fair

Going to the fair
Seeing all the rides
Going to the fair
Seeing all the lights.

Going to the fair
People all around
Going to the fair
Popcorn on the ground.

Going to the fair
People on the rides
Going to the fair
People shouting loud.

Jovan Newman Herry (8)
Sacred Heart RC Primary School

AT COURT

We're at court, we don't know what to do,
    We're rattling like a snake and so are you.
'Order! Order!' cries the judge.
    That's not true!

The judge is now banging the hammer,
    All the people are shouting.
My lawyer shouts and says, 'Objection.'
    That's not true!

The people now are sitting down,
    It's the end of court, I'm not guilty
Everybody stands and goes,
    'That's not true!'

Yohana Abraham Haile (9)
Sacred Heart RC Primary School

EVERYTHING - SOMETHING

Everything

Everything I like or dislike,
Is around me,
But how can I not like,
What my God has made?

Something

Something is not right, I think like that at night,
Is it me or something else?
Things go bump in the night,
What it is or was.

Patrick Loughney (10)
Sacred Heart RC Primary School

ALIENS

Beware of the creatures that come from above
In space or on Mars the place that I love
They are green, slimy and unwannabes
They have 3 eyes, 4 legs and 1 belly button
But where do they come from?
Nobody knows!
They could come from the sun or even Earth
Or even the planet Vados
All I know is that they come from space
The place where the little twinkly stars shine upon us
If you go there you will never come to an end,
But these creatures make our planet look a mess
They may not know
You may feel low

Declan McKenna (10)
Sacred Heart RC Primary School

MY LOVE DIARY

Your eyes are like fire, blood like rain.
Veins like a river lane.
Kiss so tender.
In the park like an angel playing a harp.
Sweet and kind, just your kind.
I say to you, 'I love you' every day.
You look in my eyes, you say to me, 'I love my sweet darling,'
You bend one knee, you say to me, 'Will you marry me?'
I cry, 'Oh yes!'
Now it's all a memory in my Love Diary.

Alexandra Louis (8)
Sacred Heart RC Primary School

CACTUS JACK IS BACK!

Bang! Bang! He's back
It's Cactus Jack.
Through the swifting wind he flows through the air
His hair waving like made in the blasting showers of the night
Bang! Bang! He's back!

Bang! Bang! He's back
It's Cactus Jack
The day so sunny, the clouds so fluffy
And Cactus blows his guns to fire
Bang! Bang! He's back! Cactus Jack.
Bang! Bang! He's back
He's riding his horse forth and back
He wins the race, he comes in first place
Bang! Bang! He's back! Cactus Jack.

Al Anthony Dipopolo (9)
Sacred Heart RC Primary School

BELLA THE CAKE MAKER

There was an old lady named Bella
She would always bake cakes in her cellar.
She could cook any cakes you desire
Like a spicy cake as hot as fire.
One day she was tired and ill
She dropped all of her smelly old pills.
She went upstairs and saw some hungry looking bears
And then she came back down to the cellar
To make some more cakes because her name was Bella.

Emma Therasa Gormley (11)
Sacred Heart RC Primary School

MY HOUSE

It is big at my house,
My mum cooks
And saw a mouse.
My house is very big
I heard a sound,
My mum told me to look
Is I looked around.
My house is very big
I heard my bell ring,
It was very loud
I heard a person sing.
My house is very big
I hear things in the air,
Like my birds
But it came from the chair.
My house is very *big!*

Andrew Olasehinde (8)
Sacred Heart RC Primary School

VALENTINE POEM

Roses are red,
Violets are blue,
Sugar is sweet,
And so are you.
When I see you my heart turns to gold,
Give me a hug, I feel so cold,
Thank you for the flowers,
Oh! The beautiful flowers,
Thank you very, very much for a lovely day.

Kristal Martin Rodrigues (10)
Sacred Heart RC Primary School

MY DOG

My dog's name's Sasha
I should have called her Thrasher
She's very mischievous
Like my Aunt Clovers
But I love her
Because she's Sasha
When we go out
We never forget her
But I love her
So let's go
But she's my dog
She loves her toy frog
And she's part of the family
Her nickname is Sally

Adam Tisseverasinghe (10)
Sacred Heart RC Primary School

THIERRY HENRY

Thierry Henry, Thierry Henry
He shoots from the left
And attacks from the right
He's like Ian Wright
And he causes lots of fright
So you'd better watch out
You'd better watch out
Because he is coming for you
He's coming for you
So get your defence ready
And get their legs ready
And prepare because he will run past them in a flash.

Charlie J Williams (10)
Sacred Heart RC Primary School

MY BIG WORRY

On one sunny, bright blue day
In the merry month of May
Me and my friends were out to play
They both tripped me and boy did they pay.

In the beautiful evening I lost my favourite shoe
I swear I knew they were two days new
When the shoe went missing I went hyper too
And I can't remember when I went to the loo.

I've got over my big worry
And started eating my curry
Now they call me a dimp
But they're the real wimp!

Ann-Marie Egan (9)
Sacred Heart RC Primary School

FRANCE

In France I had a lovely dance
It was under a branch of a tree
With lovely roses
There were loads of roses.

I had loads of ice cream
It was like my dream had come true
I saw the lovely blue sky
It looked so high
We had done some lovely things
I would always see the lovely sun.

I would always look out of the door
It would never be rainy and pour.

Daniel John Magner (9)
Sacred Heart RC Primary School

MY VERY LONG DAY

I woke up in the morning
It was a very fine day
My friend came and knocked for me
And asked me to play
I went out and played with her
And the sky was bright and blue
Then we walked passed a man
Who had a very bad flu
We walked to the gate
And saw my other mate Kate
Kate said, 'I am only eight
And I am going on a date.'
I said to Kate, 'I hope it's great.'
At the park I found a ball
Kate said, 'It is big,' but I thought it was small
At the end I went home to bed
On my own.

Cristina Narciso (8)
Sacred Heart RC Primary School

SCHOOL POEM

It's noisy in the playground,
But indoors,
There's not a sound.

Out of the window we see cars,
But we need to concentrate,
On getting stars!

'Oh no, I'm late!'
I was too slow,
Getting through the gate!

William O'Mahoney (10)
Sacred Heart RC Primary School

THE FOOTBALL MATCH

The ref giving people red cards
The crowd going wild
And the fans saying,
'Come on you reds!'

The players scoring goals
And people singing
And the fans cussing the ref
And the crowd say,
'Come on you reds!'

You see the people saying,
'Come on Arsenal, come on.'
And the crowd waving their hands saying,
'Come on you reds!'

Fenan Emanuel (9)
Sacred Heart RC Primary School

CRICKET

Cricket is boring
You end up snoring.
You get out when you run
But that's the fun.
Red balls are small
They're very hard
Not a thing to discard.
You wear a hat
When you bat
And when you field
You wear a sun shield.
All in all it is such fun
Because I like to run.

Michele Swalens (11)
Sacred Heart RC Primary School

A GOAL!

It has two posts,
One crossbar,
Someone to defend it,
And a net.

It gets hit in the arms,
Hit in the shoulder,
Hit in the head,
Hit in the chest,
Hit in the stomach,
It's always injured.

It never moves,
It only moves when there is a striking shot,
It gets a headache when people say,
　'Goaaaaaalllll!'

Paul Olasehinde (10)
Sacred Heart RC Primary School

LOVE RECIPE

Some leaves from the trees
And a little bit of breeze
Egg and tomato and cheddar cheese
Eight single daffodils
Some grass from the fields
A rabbit from a hat
A cricket bat
A sugar pile
A wonderful beating heart
Another heart that's torn apart
Stir and mix one, two, three
To make a love recipe for you and me.

Sharifa Daley (10)
Sacred Heart RC Primary School

GOING TO THE PARK

We are going to the park today, come on,
Going to the park,
We are going to have a nice time today, come on,
And it's going to be good and fun,
Going to the park.

Put your shoes on, come on,
Going to the park,
Put your jacket on, come on,
Going to the park.

Undo your laces and then do them up,
Going to the park,
Pack up your lunch, are you ready?
Here we go,
And off they went to the park,
Going to the park,
Oh, put your seat belt on,
Going to the park.

Newman Munza (8)
Sacred Heart RC Primary School

A DAY WITH THE PONIES

Ponies love to gallop,
Ponies love to jump,
Over hedges, over gates,
Or any old tree stump.

You can hear them coming,
With a whinny and a neigh,
Gallop, gallop, gallop,
Every single day.

After that the ponies love,
To have a little rest,
We brush their manes and tails,
So they can look their best.

Then they eat their carrots,
Their apples and their hay,
Munch, munch, munch,
Every single day.

Louise Harris (8)
Sacred Heart RC Primary School

BABIES

When babies are asleep,
There is not a peep.
But when they are awake,
Oh what a noise they make.

First they start to crawl,
And try to chase a ball.
Soon after they can walk,
And then they can talk.

They will go to school one day,
Then at break they start to play.
When at home,
They have to write a poem.

One day they will be grown up,
And might win the FA Cup.
Sadly they will die,
And go up to that place in the sky.

Anna O'Mahoney (8)
Sacred Heart RC Primary School

A POTION FOR SOME LOTION

We need legs from a frog
And three mounds of logs

A pinch of wind and fire
To make the consequences dire
For your face a bit of paste
Leave it to me to set you free
Add some pumpkin, the heraldee pumpkins

Get my spoon
The big golden spoon
My name is Mandy
Ha, I mean Sandy

The apple blinds the eye and the egg swishes the head
When you try this lotion
Your life will turn around
You won't feel old and bitter
You'll just look ugly with glitter

Chloe Sintim (10)
Sacred Heart RC Primary School

GARDENS

My garden's got flowers
Your garden's got towers.
My garden's got trees
Your garden's got bees.

My garden's got rope
Your garden's got soap.
I've got cats in my garden
I've got bats in my garden.

I've got a wing
I've got a ring
I fell
I've got a bell.

I've got to do more around the house
I've got a zoo
You're a fool
This is a rule.

Muna Salad Mohamed (8)
Sacred Heart RC Primary School

PARTY TIME!

People dancing on the floor,
People queuing at the door,
People talking all night long,
They're all singing to a song.

Party Time!

DJs rapping all in rhyme,
People don't even notice the time.
Lights are flashing all around,
'I'm really enjoying the sound.'

Party Time!

Time is up,
I drink my cup of Coke,
I tell my friends a little joke
And then I grab my coat.

Party Time!

Leah Kiernan (9)
Sacred Heart RC Primary School

THE EXPLORING HORSE OF COURSE

There was a horse that lived in town
That had a frown,
Then went to the shop
To buy some pop
And didn't know what to do.

There was a horse that lived in a village
Then fell off a bridge
Then went back to dry ground
And looked around
And didn't know what to do.

There was a horse that lived in the city
What a pity
So he went back home
To brush his hair with a comb
And then didn't know what to do.

There was a horse that lived in a house
Then got killed by a mouse
And didn't know what to do, *ping*
Oh yeah *nothing!*
And that's all folks!

Michael Moloney (9)
Sacred Heart RC Primary School

WHY DOES IT RAIN?

Why does it rain?
It just goes down the drain,
And drives business people totally insane,
It causes heavy traffic and makes people dramatic,
So people open up your umbrellas.

Nika Chloe Bailey (10)
Sacred Heart RC Primary School

BAD BOY TIM

Bad boy Tim is a very bad boy
He likes to tell so many lies
It's not fair, everybody said
'Bad boy Tim.'

At school he's even worse
He will even tell lies to the teachers
But still he doesn't get his way but they say
'Bad boy Tim.'

Tim is such a pain in the neck
That everybody will be sick with a headache
If they see him they will run
Bad boy Tim.

But it's even worse at home
He likes to tell bad jokes
He's such a quirk
Bad boy Tim.

Oghenekome Igoh (9)
Sacred Heart RC Primary School

MY BIRTHDAY

Remember, remember the 5th of December
The night that I was born
I was born in the Whittington hospital
And the nurse was eating corn
My mum's name's Tina
And my dad's name's Joe,
And he's a window cleaner
I've got a dog called Molly
And a cat called Polly.

Danielle Hickey (10)
Sacred Heart RC Primary School

How To Enjoy Life

When the sun is shining on my face,
I know that I have had some fun.

I have some friends,
That will make sure I have a new trend.

When I'm smiling happily,
I meet someone that makes me happy.

Try and do things you've never done before,
Therefore you will make a good sportsman.

Your life isn't over,
So put all the bad things over your shoulder.

Your life circle is what gave you talent,
So make sure it is definitely balanced.

Do things with your family that will make you happy,
So your dreams won't come with a sting.

Don't think you're a failure, so always be proud,
So don't let bullies push you around,
So stick up for yourself.

Tamaszina Jacobs-Abiola (10)
Sacred Heart RC Primary School

A Witch's Brew

A witch's broom, a new caloon,
An old man's bat, a witch's brat,
A pirate's battle, an Adam's apple,
An old man's trolley, a frilly brolly,
Sopping eyes, a pack of lies,
A piece of pear, if you dare!

Siobhan O'Sullivan (10)
Sacred Heart RC Primary School

MILLENNIUM POEM

More new centuries,
More new years,
And don't forget, no more tears.

No more racism,
No more fear,
No more battles every year.

No more battering,
No more war,
I'll ask the soldier's to give peace to the poor.

No more killing,
No more crimes,
No more destroying coal mines.

No more destroying the environment,
No more polluting the air,
No more destroying animals homes, because it is not fair.

John McIntyre (10)
Sacred Heart RC Primary School

A MAGICAL DREAM

Come with me on a magical dream
I'll take you as far as the eye can see
You say it's impossible
That's what it seems
Come with me on a magical dream
If you come you will see
It's not as impossible as it seems
Come with me on a magical dream
And then you'll believe me!

Rosie Meola (10)
Sacred Heart RC Primary School

MOANY TOMMY

Moany Tommy, Moany Tommy
He's in our school
And when we went swimming
He moaned about the pool.

Moany Tommy, Moany Tommy
He's the moaniest
When we went to the aquarium
He moaned about the fish.

Moany Tommy, Moany Tommy
He always seems to moan
When he came round my house
He moaned about my phone.

Moany Tommy, Moany Tommy
He's so moany
When the new girl came to school
She kicked him in the knee.

Connor Kilbride (10)
Sacred Heart RC Primary School

RAIN

Rain, rain it's such a pain,
Please, oh please go down the drain.
We have no time to stand and stare,
Now look what you've done to my hair.
My mother said to come straight in,
And put the rubbish in the bin.
I'm very bored, can't go and play,
Because it's been raining all through the day.

Jahleesza Jacobs-Abiola (9)
Sacred Heart RC Primary School

AT A BASKETBALL MATCH

Lots of players on the pitch
Lots of jumping up and down
Lots of cheering everywhere
Go Michael Jordan!

The ball is in the net
Lots of shouting everywhere
'Foul,' shouts the ref
Go Michael Jordan!

Happy people all around
Waving hands 'cause they have won
'We've won, we've won,' they shout with joy
Go Michael Jordan!

It's time to go home
We've had a good day
The whole lot of us get on the bus
Go Michael Jordan!

James Jordan (8)
Sacred Heart RC Primary School

SCHOOL!

It's 9 o'clock and we hear the bell ring
It's time for school with Mr Ping
We're working hard with closing eyes
Our dreams come true at 10:35
We're having lunch which is not very nice
We hear the kitchen is full of mice
It's 3:30 and loud cheers will ring
Once we hear the final bell ting.

Danny Colclough (10)
Sacred Heart RC Primary School

BE A MONSTER

I am a frightful monster
My face is cabbage green
And even with my mouth shut
My teeth can still be seen
My fingernails are like rats' tails
And very far from clean.

I cannot speak a language
But make a wailing sound
It would be any corner
You find me coming round
The arms outspread and eyeballs red
I skim across the ground.

The girls scream out, 'Scatter
From this girl-eating a bat.'
I usually catch a small one
Because her legs are fat;
Or maybe she's tricked by me
Wearing her grandpa's hat.

Abigail Owusu (10)
Sacred Heart RC Primary School

MATILDA

Who told lies and was burnt to death?
Matilda told such dreadful lies
It made one gasp and stretch one's eyes
Her aunt from her earliest youth
Had strict regard for truth
Attempted to believe Matilda
The effort nearly killed her.

Aaron Chesterman (10)
Sacred Heart RC Primary School

BED BUGS IN THE NIGHT

Bed bugs scratching
Bed bugs biting
Bed bugs in the night
In your bed shouting
When they give you a fright
Shout to your mum
And make some rum
Bed bugs in the night
Bed bugs shouting when they are fat
With us jumping on the bed
Bed bugs in the night
Help! Help! Help!
I don't
Know
What
To
Do.

Molly Doyle (9)
Sacred Heart RC Primary School

IP DIP ON THE WALL

Ip dip on the wall
Don't climb the wall or you'll fall
Just because your ball got kicked on the wall
Ip dip on the wall
Don't go on your shoulders to get your ball
Because it got kicked on the wall
Ip dip on the wall

Chinedu Nwachuku (10)
Sacred Heart RC Primary School

HELP! HELP! HELP!

I'm in a bad mood today
I'm playing the Nintendo
And can't get past level five
And I'm jumping on the floor

I'm in a bad mood today
I feel really mad
If I could bite, kick or punch something
It would make me feel so glad

I'm in a bad mood today
I've fought with everyone
I was cheeky to my mum
I said she had a big fat bum

She tapped me on my head
And told me and my bad mood
To go to bed

Dannii Docherty (9)
Sacred Heart RC Primary School

SLAVES

Slaving away night and day
Working for master's crown.
One day I think
I am going to let him down.
We have to do everything
Just for master's sake.
We have to do all jobs
Like farming with a rake.
One day I shall run away
And have a holiday.

Frances K M Lasok (7)
Sacred Heart RC Primary School

130

WHAT IS AT THE FOOTBALL MATCH

The fans with painted faces
Cheering for their team
The whistle blows for half time
Go Arsenal!

The fans do the Mexican wave
The people screaming loudly
The whistle blows again
Go Arsenal!

People eating and drinking
See people fight badly
There goes the final whistle
Go Arsenal!

Sandra Atim Okidi (9)
Sacred Heart RC Primary School

WHAT A DAY AT THE PARK

I went to the park
To play with my bat
It began to rain
So I put on my hat.

Silly old me, I stayed there too long
And because of this I saw a rat
Me, myself I hate all rat kinds
So I hit it with a baseball bat.

Then I rushed home
And I gasped
I said to myself,
'I'd better not ask.'

Matthew Ward (8)
Sacred Heart RC Primary School

AT A DANCING LESSON

People dancing on the floor
The teacher saying, 'Stop that now!'
People singing to the music
Dancing lessons are the best.

Girls wearing dresses, boys wearing trousers
The teacher says, 'Get a partner!'
Boys and girls dancing madly
Dancing lessons are the best.

The radio bouncing in the air
Kid saying, 'I feel sea sick.'
At the end boys kissing the girls goodbye
Dancing lessons are the best.

Adèle Martini (9)
Sacred Heart RC Primary School

A PARTY

A party is good, a party is good
We should boogie it all night long
We should dance until we fall
It's so much fun
I will show them how to dance
I am gonna shake it all night long

Don't be scared, you're gonna do the ooga booga yeah!
So come here and be a fantastic man
Yes! You hear the song play very loud
Yes! The karaoke is on, you can sing a song
You favourite song
Come on
What are you gonna do dance. *Yes.*

Tommy McInerney (9)
Sacred Heart RC Primary School

The Basketball Match

The fans are eating hot dogs
Cheering loudly for their team
The players are passing fast
And suddenly
Bang! Another goal

I see the goals being scored
I hear the ball bouncing loudly
A player is running and dribbling
And then
Baaang! Another goal

The court is full with people
I hear steps from the player
Running speedily,
There's only five minutes to go
Bang! Another goal

Alexander Demosthenous (9)
Sacred Heart RC Primary School

School

'Daddy why do we have to go to school?'
'Oh just shut up and go to bed.'
'Oh dear Daddy there are people always calling us names
And it always continues.'
'Now go to bed.'
'Oh dear Daddy the reading books to me are boring.'
'Just shut up and go to bed.'
'And dear Daddy I wonder why the school building
Is so creepy, Daddy?'
'Just shut up and go to bed dear.'

Ngozi Osuala (10)
Sacred Heart RC Primary School

I HAVE A CAT CALLED PIPPA

I have a cat called Pippa
She is so nice and sweet
And when you take your shoes off
She comes and smells your feet.

I have a cat called Pippa
She loves eating her food
But when you come to play with her
She starts acting rather rude.

I have a cat called Pippa
She loves it when she sleeps,
Pippa's got bright yellow eyes
And she daydreams of little sheep.

Pippa has got lovely fur
And when you stroke her she will purr
She will chew on your slipper
I have a cat called Pippa.

Natalie Maznik (9)
Sacred Heart RC Primary School

WE GET PLAY

The children come to school
Next the bell rings
Everybody goes inside
We get play!

We read a story
Then we start work
A few minutes later
We get play!

We meet our friends
Friends are fun
We make up games
We get play!

The whistle blows
Time to line up
Now it's home time
We get play!

Adam Sas (8)
Sacred Heart RC Primary School

ODE TO A GHOST

A ghost has a sad old life
Haunting empty castles
On birthdays and on Christmases
A postman brings no parcels.

He floats around from room to room
He howls and clanks his chains
But everyone ignores the noise
And blames it on the drains.

And if by chance he should appear
Most people scream with fright
He just could not understand
Is he such a dreadful sight?

He has no one to play with
It really is a shame
He would like to come round to tea
Or join you in a game.

Oladele Ayodele (10)
Sacred Heart RC Primary School

SCHOOL

S chool is boring, school is bad,
  head teacher sick, all we need losing money, we can't feed.
C an't concentrate with the builders so get rid of them
  And bring back the teachers.
H ow come football's banned?
  Never mind, we'll kick a can around.
O ur school is big, our school is small
  I don't care, we got it all.
O ur school smells
  It could destroy my brain cells.
L ook around, hear the sound . . .
  Total silence, children have gone.

Daniel Flynn (10)
Sacred Heart RC Primary School

SUNNY SKY

Sun shining in the sky
Lighter than a magpie.
Pass smoothly through the air
Making tracks here and there.
The sun brings love, laughter and light
But! Then came the rain, sad and angry.
The sun tired to fight - bish bash,
Thunder, lighting and finally there was silence.
The sun won the battle and a rainbow came in the sky.
The sun was happy again.

Elizabeth Mitchell-Yankah (11)
Sacred Heart RC Primary School

CHANGING WEATHER

Crescent moon, star bright
Rain falls, dark night
Are you wet from that shower?
A new sunrise lights my day
Feel the warm summer breeze
Flowing and blowing.

Stephen Grieve (9)
Sacred Heart RC Primary School

MY FAMILY

Hi, I'm Sasha and this is my mum,
And we both like chewing gum,
I have a big family but no one can tell,
Most of my family is tall
But I am the only one
That turned out small.

Sasha Wickham (10)
Sacred Heart RC Primary School

EMINEM

E   minem is the best rapper in the world
M   ay I add he had a really hard life
I   think he should not be banned anywhere
N   o hard feeling 'Em' but
E   minem calm down on your words
M   ay I rest my case, goodbye.

Claudio Narciso (11)
Sacred Heart RC Primary School

AT THE FOOTBALL MATCH

The fans have painted faces
Cheering loudly for their team
The whistle blows for half-time
    Go Arsenal Go!

The players kicking the ball
The fans singing, 'Come on, come on.'
The fans are clapping excitedly
    Go Arsenal Go!

The ref blowing the whistle
Crowds are waving happily
Hooray! The Reds just scored
    Go Arsenal Go!

The ball being kicked quickly
Oh no! The Blues just scored
The Reds moaning at the Blues
    Go Arsenal Go!

Katie Louise O'Connor (9)
Sacred Heart RC Primary School

LIGHTNING

Lightning, lightning
It's so frightening
That big flash
Makes me dash
I run and hide
Quickly inside

Lightning, lightning
In the dark it's so brightening
That big strike
It's what I like
It can be scary
Like my friend Mary

Conor O'Toole (9)
Sacred Heart RC Primary School

MYSELF

Here's a poem about myself
I have no furniture
I have no shelf
In Mum's bedroom
I love her curtains
In Dad's bedroom
I am not too certain
I am always thinking about the world I like
Being fun is just my type
Somehow, somewhere I should maybe
In a garden of apple trees
I have no house, I have no phone
Sometimes I wish I am home alone
I have finish, friends and family
I shouldn't say I am glad to be their uncles and aunties
Isn't it true, it's me?
My life is a big disappointment sometimes
I regret I was born, away from the fire
Or I'll roast like a corn
My days are a tragedy
Yes you could see when Mum shouts
While my dad's holding me.

Charlotte Ireca Aaron Pryce (10)
St Francesca Cabrini Primary School

IN THE PLAYGROUND

In the playground is a big huffle,
On the floor all the feet shuffle.
Children dance, laugh and play,
While I just sit and watch them all day.
Sometimes I see ropes flying in the air,
With the person's hair flying everywhere.
The sound of laughter runs through my ears,
Like your finger going through water.
But there's just nothing there.
They play racing games and football and tennis too,
As they go running, and the balls fly
People are cheering, and waiting for a goal.
The children laugh and play even more.
As the bell goes everybody runs to their line with a great big bustle.

Jade Louise O'Shea (9)
St Francesca Cabrini Primary School

THE WORLD

The world is big, green and blue
There's people all over the country like you
The world is round, big and blue
The world is full of people for you
The world is full of fun for humans like you
No need for you humans to be afraid
The world is with you every step of the way
The world is as friendly as your best friend
You can always count on the world when you need it
Don't be afraid of it, trust it.

Lauren Monique Simone Bamford-Vivien (11)
St Francesca Cabrini Primary School

MY FAMILY

My family is soooo into sport,
My mum and dad run a mile a day
My brother plays football every Saturday
He even broke my bedroom window
My dad doesn't even care that I'm sleeping in a cold and damp room
My mum is too busy on the exercise machine
What is a girl my age supposed to do?
Call the police?
If I call the police, mum and dad will be sent away
And who will look after me?
My brother Michael?
Strange life for a 9-year-old.

What is a girl my age supposed to do?

Martha Rubondo (9)
St Francesca Cabrini Primary School

TOPCAT

There once was a cat with a hat
It was called Topcat
It lived in the trash
It made a clash
Every time he would eat trash
There was a bash and a clash
So Topcat got out of his trash can
And he clashed and he bashed it with a hammer
So it did not make a difference
So he got a truck and crunched the can of rubbish.

Aidan Lee Robert Coates (11)
St Francesca Cabrini Primary School

I WORK IN HEAVEN

My name is Blessing; I work in Heaven,
I start at nine and I finish at seven.
I work with Daniel, David and Moses,
We work in the Lord's garden collecting roses.
We lay the roses on the heavenly path,
Then David runs the water for Jesus to bath.
Heaven is filled with beautiful light clouds,
And angels singing praises aloud.
Heaven is so comfortable and filled with love,
And is also filled with little white doves.
At lunchtime we go to the heavenly hall,
Collect our lunches and sit around Paul.
Paul prays for us and tells us about Jesus,
Then gives us all a packet of Maltesers.
We got to the Lord's centre to give some care,
To people who are old and have no hair.
It is seven o'clock; I have to go home,
Heaven is where I live, my home sweet home.

Blessing Okereafor (10)
St Francesca Cabrini Primary School

THE NINE PLANETS

The nine planets in the solar system,
Sway and dance around the sun
Bumping into each other
Always touching the sun
But one day Pluto crashed into the sun,
And blew up in the planet's face.
Now there are only eight planets left
Which sway and dance in space.

Daniel Faluyi (9)
St Francesca Cabrini Primary School

EARTH

As round as a ball
As blue as the sky
Why oh why do we have to say bye bye?
Why not take Mars, Neptune or Saturn?
Why oh why does it have to die?
We all live on it
We all die on it
Why can't we die on it, not it die on us?
If it says bye bye so do we
Why not stay for another day?
Round and round we go every day
Why can't it stay?
I'm hating the day it has to go
There's nothing we can do
There's nothing we can show
To stop it going away

James Flowerday (11)
St Francesca Cabrini Primary School

THE NET

I kick the ball hard in the net
The cold ground jumps up
I soon will still be sitting down
With a deep frown
I wonder what is going on?
I stand on my warm seat
My shoes come off my tired feet
I climb over everyone
I slip with thump! Bump! Bump! Bump!

Billy Rutherwood (9)
St Francesca Cabrini Primary School

MY PILLOW

My pillow is squashy and soft,
My mum always keeps it in the loft,
But I always go and get it out,
And I end up eating all my sprouts.

I cannot sleep without my pillow,
And without the story of the willow,
Would you wish to have a pillow like mine,
So you can sleep and let it shine?

I wish my pillow was magical,
So it could take me places,
Like *Disneyland,*
And a beach with all the sand.

Wendy Bediako (10)
St Francesca Cabrini Primary School

SURPRISES

Surprises go bang and boom!
Surprises appear in your room,
You never know what's inside,
It could even be a dusty old broom.

Surprises are birthday parties,
Surprises are a gift to learn karate,
You're always grateful for what you get,
Even if it's a pack of Smarties.

Surprises are full of laughter,
Surprises have lots of crafters,
It could be a present or a shock,
But most of all it's best after.

Raffaela Piscina (10)
St Francesca Cabrini Primary School

SUNSET FEAST

The sky went orange, red and yellow.
It was a beauty, it was a sight.
Crowds were gathered around the beach,
Waiting for the sun to set.

Fishing men come in, some fishing men go out,
People gather around a fire,
And put today's catch on a stove,
Women and children and families bring out herbs
And sprinkle them over the meal.

As the sun sets so calmly,
People share their food around.
Fine chefs of the village bring their finest wine,
And everyone enjoys their sunset feast.

Victoria Reese (10)
St Francesca Cabrini Primary School

I LOVE ICE CREAM

I love ice cream, it never makes me scream
It wriggles down my belly
All swormy like jelly
I lick it, I lick it, I lick it
It never makes me sick
An ice cream can handle its own taste
So don't leave it in a waste
Pick ice cream
Don't let it go
When you lick it
Lick it slow.

Sandra Birungi (9)
St Francesca Cabrini Primary School

MY QUEEN

My queen is so fat,
And she lives in a flat,
She has a noisy dog,
And he's called Mog.

No one comes knocking on her door,
Because she has a very loud roar!

She is so dumb,
That she sucks her thumb,
She likes to eat lime,
Every single time.

Beware of the queen,
She might give you a scream.

Damilola Ikeola (9)
St Francesca Cabrini Primary School

HAPPINESS IS . . .

Happiness is on Christmas.
Happiness is on my birthday.
Happiness is when it is sunny.
Happiness is going to my friend's house.
Happiness is going to a party.
Happiness is laughing.
Happiness is drawing a picture.
Happiness is at Easter.
Happiness is playing at home.
Happiness is when people let you play with them.

Jodie Finch (7)
St Francesca Cabrini Primary School

THE VERY HOT SUN

It is very hot
But I don't care
Because it's my type
Nothing else.

It's as bright as a star
As big as space
As wide as a tree
As red as Eugene's cheeks
As hot as a fire.

There's nothing better than the sun
Only football of course
There's nothing better than the sun
Only cricket of course.

Joseph Patrick Quinn (10)
St Francesca Cabrini Primary School

ANGER IS . . .

Anger is when you are blamed.
Anger is when you do your homework badly.
Anger is when you have school.
Anger is when you are bored.
Anger is when you have nobody to play with.
Anger is when you have to tidy up your room.
Anger is when your mum shouts at you.
Anger is when you make a mistake.
Anger is when I snap my pencils.
Anger is when I lose a friend.

Nicholas Okraku (7)
St Francesca Cabrini Primary School

FACES

What do you see when you look at faces
around you?

Do you see . . .
> Happy faces, sad faces
> Angry faces, calm faces
> Smiling, cross or wrinkly faces?

What do they tell:
> A sulky face on a demanding toddler not allowed sweets.
> Shifty faces which hide deep dark secrets.
> Proud faces of the successful students.
> Delighted faces on the winning football team.
> Dismayed faces on the losing football team.
> Wrinkly faces full of mysterious history.

Think about the faces you have seen today . . .

Think about what they mean . . .

. . . What does yours say?

Rebecca D'Costa (9)
St Francesca Cabrini Primary School

FAMILY

F   amily is important,
A   ll of them love you, no matter what you do.
M   ums are caring, loving, sharing and so are all the rest of your family.
I   love my family very, very much and I'm sure you do too.
L   ove is very important so share it with your family members.
Y   ou are loved by all of your family and they are loved by you.
> Family is important so take care of them and treat them with
respect.

Rachel Victoria Kearns (10)
St Francesca Cabrini Primary School

THE SOLAR SYSTEM

The planets glazing through the night
Bumping into each other without any main fights.
Neptune, Saturn and Venus prepare a vicious game
That has always been the same.
Mercury, Mars and Jupiter noisy their heads
Inside the beds.
Three of them giggle, jiggle and wriggle
By telling Uranus, Pluto and Earth to circle around the moon
                                                    for attention.
Neptune, Saturn and Venus come pushing six of them
Fun, fun how could this be for these nine planets.
Suddenly *bang!*
They're gone,
Perhaps sun and moon are the only ones in the solar system.

Vicky Atutu (9)
St Francesca Cabrini Primary School

CHICAGO BULLS

I'm in Chicago,
The real cool Chicago,
I'm on the bull, the red fierce bull,
Cool as cool on the ring-pierced bull,
Scared out of my pants of the terrifying bull,
I'm in the barn with a hot, hot sweater,
Looking at the bulls with their bad, bad temper,
It's too late to run now,
'Cause The Chicago Bulls are here, red as red.

Nathaniel Brown (10)
St Francesca Cabrini Primary School

STAR OF THE SOLAR SYSTEM

There was a time when the stars ruled the sky,
And the moon ruled the solar system, planet's kingdom so high.
They all lived in a peaceful race,
And by the way they all had a beautiful face.
Then a star of the moon was born.
In happiness they blew a magic moon horn,
In which it rested in this magical place.

There were only eight planets at this time,
And there wasn't nine
Until a later time.

The hot bright star, the sun so blazing hot,
Swallowed us all!
The lovely star protected all the planets,
Apart from the meteors and all,
That the hot molten in each rock exploded,
And make a huge *bang!*
The rocks formed a planet, known now as Earth,
Everybody was happy and sang.

As we gaze from our windows,
On the new planet Earth,
We wish upon the moon star,
All our desires and wishes shall come true,
Now Heaven and Earth can rest peacefully,

And when we go we lift our bodies so Earth can go to Heaven too.

Joan Digba (9)
St Francesca Cabrini Primary School

POEM OF THE OTHER WORLD

The world is great,
It's fun too,
There are lots of things to see and do,
I think you'll like this world of mine,
Because it's new,
To all of you,
I'm not exactly what you think I am,
'Cause I am totally different in many ways,
I could give you clues,
But then it would lose,
All the fun of the game,
The game is to guess,
Where I am,
And who am I?
If you are right,
You'll have to fight,
But in the alien way,
Oh no,
I've given it away!
Ahha you still don't know who I am,
At this new world of mine,
I'll give you a clue,
About what to do,
But you'll never guess,
Where I've just landed,
In my little ship,
I don't have a clue where I am,
Some kind of other world,
Is it Earth or is it not?

Katie Doherty (11)
St Francesca Cabrini Primary School

THE COMPETITION

Poetic Voyages was the title of the sign.
First prize was £20; it had to be mine.
It's only a try, I won't write a poem too long,
It's stuck in my head, as if it's a song.
I didn't now what to say; could I write about today?
Finally, I got it done,
I had written about the sun.
In my hand there is 20 pound,
In my hand, safe and sound.
'Wake up boy, it's time for school.'
And my thought evaporated like a dried up pool.
Then it began to seem,
As if it were all a dream.
But there is a £20 note in my hand,
I could feel it now, crisp as sand.
Now I don't know what to buy,
'Let's not start this again,' I thought with a sigh.

Gerard McQuade (11)
St Francesca Cabrini Primary School

TOPMAN

I'm living large and
I'm in charge and
I'm on the top because
I know how to rock
I've got millions of dollars
I've got kids and toddlers
I've got hotels to run
I've got nightclubs to run
I've got places to go
I've got a life you know!

Nathan Bowen (11)
St Francesca Cabrini Primary School

WHAT CHILD IS THIS?

Something happened a long time ago
To Mary and Joseph on their way to go,
When they travelled from far away
Mary met with a baby where they lay,
Special people came far and wide
And when they got there, 'Oh' how they cried,
For a baby was born on that starry night
The great King himself Jesus Christ,
They all wondered, 'What child is this?'
Because he was so poor but very bliss,
They gave him frankincense, gold and myrrh
To represent his royalness and kindness occur,
Then shepherds came with one of God's gifts
To give him food and water,
Then Mary gave Jesus a gentle kiss.

Curtis G Perriman (11)
St Francesca Cabrini Primary School

HAPPINESS

Happiness is when I have fun.
Happiness is when it's sunny.
Happiness is when you smile.
Happiness is when you're not alone.
Happiness is when you go to a party.
Happiness is when something funny happens.
Happiness is when you get a good report.
Happiness is when I have someone to play with.
Happiness is when you get a treat.
Happiness is when a teacher's friendly.

Michelle Nantege (7)
St Francesca Cabrini Primary School

THE WORLD

Tropical rainforests, home of many different creatures,
And amazing waterfalls; the rushing sapphire blue,
Countries like hot India; it's most exotic features,
Could make any normal person's wildest dream come true.
A history of time, that's gone through all ages,
Seen love, hate, hope and death through all the world's stages,
Saw Moses separate the tossing Red Sea,
Saw World Wars I and II, but not III,
Saw the black slaves be set free,
From Adam and Eve's garden sorrow,
To today; where's tomorrow?
Are we fast approaching the end?
Is 2001 the very last bend?
Will the Big Bang not be that long?
Or will the world go on and on?

Helena Day (10)
St Francesca Cabrini Primary School

THERE'S A MONSTER UNDER MY BED

I walked into my bedroom, I went to sleep,
There was a noise at midnight, I looked under my sheet.
It was a monster once again, looking up at me,
So I screamed as loud a is could but no one seemed to hear me.
Then I knew why God made monsters,
So they can eat children and watch Blockbusters.
I ran downstairs at 12 o'clock, I tried to get out but the door was
lockcd.
The TV was on, I didn't care, I turned around,
The monster was there . . !

Mariam Garba (10)
St Francesca Cabrini Primary School

MONSTER UNDER MY BED

I walked into my bedroom, then ran across the floor
Because I knew something terrible - the monster, was there once more!
I knew its eyes, I knew its laugh,
I knew its teeth could cut me in half
The light's turned off, I wanted to scream
IT was meant to be reality but it was like a horrible dream
I was scared out of my wits, from head to toe
I wished the monster would just go
My TV was on, I didn't care
I turned around, the monster was there!
'I want food!' the monster roared
'And I wish you would just eat me
Because I'm getting quite bored!'

Catherine Dunn (10)
St Francesca Cabrini Primary School

THE MARKET

I go to a market which is always full.
Sometimes we eat some bull.
I go with my mum there every day,
Mostly I meet my friend and we play.
The food there is yummy, I think it is good for my tummy.
And I once met a baby bunny.
My dad is coming to visit,
I bet he brings me a toy.
It was not him! It was an old friend.
I hope he takes me to the market!
And he did.
Now he has to leave and so do I -
Goodbye!

Grace McQuade (10)
St Francesca Cabrini Primary School

THE SEA

I sit on the beach,
I look out to sea,
The sun is hot,
Shining down on me.

The sky is baby blue,
The clouds as white as snow,
I can't wait for a cool wind to blow.

The waves rush in,
Nearly touching my feet,
Oh, what a lovely day,
To sit out in the heat.

I am wearing my hat,
It's shading my face,
I'm looking for shells,
All over the place.

I've found a big shell,
I put it to my ear,
Isn't it amazing,
The things that you hear!

Someone is crying,
I look around,
Poor thing has dropped
His ice cream on the ground.

I stand in the water,
And look at the sky,
So many seagulls,
Come flying by.

The water is cool,
As I stand in the foam,
My mother is calling,
'It's time to go home.'

Daniella Salamone (10)
St Francesca Cabrini Primary School

MY KING

My king is so dumb.
He cannot play a drum.
My king is so fat.
He even has a smelly old cat.

My king loses his head
When he's being fed
In his bed.

My king listens to music
Wearing a wig.
Sometimes he likes to do the jig.

My king is so selfish.
My king is so rude.
He is always in a bad mood.

My king doesn't let you in his castle
Even if you bring him his parcel.
So watch out for the king.
He might give you a ring
Or a sting!

Alarape Ojetunde (9)
St Francesca Cabrini Primary School

NONSENSE POEM

I'm a child and I'm not wild
Some people think I am
Because I have a brain and it drives me insane.
I have a pet snake
I've never seen a lake
I think my mum's going to bake a cake.
I am nine
I don't like wine
And everything I touch must be mine.
I like to dig
Today I saw a pig
Under London Bridge.
My birthday is in May
And my hair is not grey.
I'm not ninety-nine
And I know how to draw a line.
Right now I am fine.
I have a TV and I'm older than three.

Andreas Theophani (9)
St Francesca Cabrini Primary School

FIRE AND ICE

Some say the world will end in fire
Some say in ice
From what I've tasted of desire
I hold with those who favour fire
But if it had to perish twice
I think I know enough of hate
To say that for destruction
Ice is also great
And would suffice.

Fallon Riggs-Long (8)
St Francesca Cabrini Primary School

SCARED OF . . .

If no one's scared of spiders,
If no one's scared of bees,
Why should we run under trees?

If no one's scared of barks,
If no one's scared of sharks,
Why should we scream like we're in the dark?

If you are scared of flies,
As they go by,
Don't worry because you won't cry.

If you're scared of teachers,
If you're scared of me,
Don't cry, just look at me.

If you love cats and dogs
You might like everything,
And never run away from dogs,
Else they will bite.

Michelle Oppong (8)
St Francesca Cabrini Primary School

CANDLES

If you light a candle,
It's just a little light,
But if you leave it burning,
It makes the room so bright.

When the wax is melting,
It goes drip, drip, drip,
So if you're walking past,
Mind that you don't slip!

Michaela McMahon (8)
St Francesca Cabrini Primary School

SEASONS IN ME

I like it when summer comes
I have loads of fun
Playing with friends and having picnics
Under the blazing sun

When summer ends and winter comes
The leaves begin to fall
I like to put them into piles
And kick them like a ball

Then winter comes along
Freezing, wet and cold
I spend most days tucked up indoors
Doing what I'm told

The springtime is a lovely time
When everything is new
And I can get back out again
To enjoy the things I do.

Kirsty McCaughan (10)
St Francesca Cabrini Primary School

HAPPINESS IS . . .

Happiness is winning the race.
Happiness is tying your lace.
Happiness is watching television.
Happiness is going to bed late.
Happiness is when the sun is out.
Happiness is when sweets are in your mouth.
Happiness is when it's Christmas.
Happiness is when it's your birthday.
Happiness is when your story's on the wall.

James D'Costa (8)
St Francesca Cabrini Primary School

BEST FRIENDS

My friend is very crazy
She's driving me blazy
Her name is Josephine Lee
She says, 'Where's my key?'

My name is Leanne Cater
She says, 'See you later.'
She's coming to my birthday party
In Bromley on Saturday
But her birthday's in May.

We both come from Ireland
Yes Ireland is the place
When we're in Ireland
We can see each other's face.

She comes from Galway
I come from Kildare
She says in Kildare
There's a flood there.

Leanne Cater (8)
St Francesca Cabrini Primary School

IMAGINE

Image there's no shops
Imagine there's no trees
Imagine there's no animals
Imagine there's no food
Imagine there's no sea
Imagine there's no people
Imagine there's nothing

Priscilla Owusu Ansah (10)
St Francesca Cabrini Primary School

An Old Lady

There was an old lady from Cork,
Who wanted to fly like a hawk,
She made herself wings from blankets and things,
And flew all the way to New York.

She waited and waited for a 63 to come,
People pointed and stared and thought she was dumb.

The 63 bus never came,
So she took a Broadway train,
She fell asleep and ended up in Spain,
The pain was too much, she ended up with a broken back.

It was now time to go,
Her back felt sore,
She packed up her things and put on her wings,
And ended her life with a broken back.

Tobi Odumosu (9)
St Francesca Cabrini Primary School

Love

Happiness is when I do well.
Happiness is when I'm happy.
Happiness is when my mum is proud of me.
Happiness is when I have friends.
Happines is when I'm trusted.
Happiness is when people love one another.
Happiness is when we are kind to one another.
Happiness is when someone looks after you.
Happiness is when your teacher is proud of you.
Happiness is when it's sunny.

Daniela Tome (8)
St Francesca Cabrini Primary School

BEING A TWIN

Being a twin can be fun
If you have a fun twin.

It will feel exciting
If you have an exciting twin.

You can feel loved 24 hours a day
If you have a loveable twin.

You can feel not alone
If you a have a twin who knows they are not alone.

You can feel cool
If you have a cool twin.

And my twin sister, Taiwo has all of that
So for me
I love being a twin.

Kehinde Sotonwa (10)
St Francesca Cabrini Primary School

I HAVE A DOG

I have a dog,
It barks at me,
It steps,
It eats,
It follows me,
It climbs me,
It licks me,
I go to the park with her.

Nana Gyan-Apenteng
St Francesca Cabrini Primary School

WHO AM I?

E   dward is my name.
D   rawing is my fourth best hobby.
W   WF is my best wrestling programme.
A   boy who is helpful.
R   eading is one of my hobbies.
D   oing tennis is my best hobby.

A   ndoh is the first bit of my surname.
N   ever jealous.
D   odzie is the last bit of my surname.
O   ut of my family I am the youngest.
H   aving to be a male is good.

D   eadly diseases are my best book.
A   boy who is funny.
D   ogs are fast.
Z   ebras are one of the animals I want to see.
I   come from Ghana.
E   is the first letter of my whole name.

Edward Andoh-Dadzie (8)
St Francesca Cabrini Primary School

THE MOON

The atmosphere is so still and quiet
It's almost like a party riot.
When a man first lay foot on the moon
All he saw was craters and gloom.
When you look at it at night
It lights up like a sight of fright.
The moon is so interesting
It makes me feel so.

Bradley Davies (11)
St Francesca Cabrini Primary School

LISA

There was a girl called Lisa
Her favourite food was pizza
Her best friend's name was Eva
And she was a disco diva.

Her dad's friend's name was Tony
And he always rode his pony
He also had a hamster
Who unfortunately had cancer.

Tony's tiny hamster
Who had brain cancer
After Lisa went to Dover
She actually came over.

But when she came
She acted so lame
The poor hamster died
And Lisa never came back again.

Eva Adekunle (10)
St Francesca Cabrini Primary School

HAPPINESS IS . . .

Happiness is a surprise.
Happiness is a surprise party.
Happiness is when it's sunny.
Happiness is the summer holidays.
Happiness is when you're proud.
Happiness is fun.
Happiness is when your football team wins.
Happiness is when you play.
Happiness is when someone's proud of me.

Jerome Dalphinis (7)
St Francesca Cabrini Primary School

THE HAUNTED HOUSE

A nna lives in an old haunted house,
N o one knows what it's like in there.
N o one knows what else might live in there
A nd there might even be a man-eating mouse!

G rowing ivy and moss all around
R ound the back there's a howling hound.
I n the window there's a grandfather clock
M aybe it's stopped, going tick tock!
A ll this time she's had that house
L ong years ago it was made.
D are someone to knock on the door!
I n the pathway to the house they would always ignore!

Anna Grimaldi (9)
St Francesca Cabrini Primary School

THE HAUNTED HOUSE

B reanne lives in an old haunted house
R ipped wallpaper
E choing hallways
A ncient statues
N ever go near the garden
N ever go near the weeds
E ven the front door is haunted

L anterns are used instead of lights
A nd lights have been invented
W hat an old-fashioned person!
L eave the pathway plants alone
O r they might jump out and grab you
R un away from the house, never go near it again.

Breanne Lawlor (9)
St Francesca Cabrini Primary School

ANIMAL ADVENTURE

My pig looks funny in wigs
A piranha drinks lager.
Lions eat meat
And hamsters are sweet.

Birds are nerds
A lizard can give you a fright
Even when it's bright.
Rattlesnakes make little earthquakes
A fox fits nicely in a box.

A whale has a nice shiny tail
A shark plays in a park.
Cats eat rats
And dogs' poo on logs.

Kleo Joseph (9)
St Francesca Cabrini Primary School

MY BEST FRIEND

My best friend drives me crazy
And sometimes he's lazy.
He talks about girls
And he says he wants painted nails,
He's very, very crazy.
He says his name is Take
But his name is Jake.
Sometimes he's nice and sometimes he's bad.
He talks about elephants,
He talks about football
And Jake likes football so do I
We called it Tool Football.

Kieron Pryce (8)
St Francesca Cabrini Primary School

MYSELF

D   aniela is
A   lways friendly
N   ever rude
I   s always helpful
E   ats chocolate and crisps
L   oves my family
A   lways clean

C   leans and cares for one another
O   ften reading
F   eels great every day
O   ften eating
N   ever swears
E   ats what I'm given

Daniela Cofone (9)
St Francesca Cabrini Primary School

WORK

Sometimes work is boring
Can't we once just do drawing?

Hey! Music is quite fun
Dum dum de dum

Oh maths, maths, maths
You know it is a little daft

And teachers are just preachers
About work!

Isabelle Goldrick (8)
St Francesca Cabrini Primary School

NEVER KEEPING PROMISES!

I asked my friend to come and play ball, she said . . .
'Yes! Never ! Never! Never!'

I asked my mum to help me with my homework, she said . . .
'Yes! Never! Never! Never!'

I was going mad, silly, crazy, I can't explain it.

I asked my grandad if he had any medicine for going mad,
He said . . . 'I don't know!
Never! Never ! never!'

Mia-Sara Crowther-Nicol (8)
St Francesca Cabrini Primary School

THE BOAT

The boat is very big.
It has lots of things on board.
It has ropes and an engine and it's even called the Wasp.
Stuart Little drives the boat in the race.
George even calls him to win the race.
Stuart always watches out for trouble and even tries to win the race.
At the end he won the race and he got a trophy.
So they celebrated and the family couldn't believe the story.
He got taken away from the Little's by Mr and Mrs Stoat.
They got into many dangers on the back to the Little's
But he got back eventually.

Christopher Smyth (9)
St Francesca Cabrini Primary School

FRIENDSHIP AND FEELINGS

Friendship and feelings
Are special things you know.
Friends know what it means
I don't know about foes.
Different people like different things
So probably foes don't like friendship.
My best friend is a very good girl
I think she's the best girl in the whole wide world.
When I'm not feeling well she's always there for me,
She makes me so, so full of glee.

Beryl Sagay (9)
St Francesca Cabrini Primary School

A SURPRISE

A surprise is when it is my birthday.
A surprise is when I get to go to the park.
A surprise is whenI go on a trip.
A surprise is when I get a present.
A surprise is when I get a slap.
A surprise is when I am good at school.
A surprise is when I make my mummy and daddy happy.

Adriana Loaiza Villagomez (7)
St Francesca Cabrini Primary School

THE MOON

Moon, moon I love the way you shine,
You make me happy when I look at you.
When you shine you shine so sweet,
But how you look is the best of all.

Anna-Maria Neophytou (9)
St Francesca Cabrini Primary School

MY FRIEND

My friend takes my pencils and calls me names
And play fights with me but he's not like that at my house.
At my friend's house he plays jump on his bed
We like to jump on my friends bed
But I don't like my friend at school
He calls me names and takes my pencils
And play fights with me
But I like my friend at his house.

James Jones (9)
St Francesca Cabrini Primary School

THE ACROBAT

C   aroline is an
A   crobat.
R   ound, round
O   ver and over
L   ike a monkey.
I   would want to be a champion.
N   ow I'm in training.
E   nd of my poem.

Caroline Svensson (9)
St Francesca Cabrini Primary School

MY FRIEND

Sometimes I feel that something isn't right in my heart
And sometimes I hear my friend say something
Something I don't like.
Sometimes we become friends again
And sometimes we get mad with each other.

Conall Garland-Harkin (8)
St Francesca Cabrini Primary School

HOMEWORK

H omework is not for kids,
O ften we leave it and it becomes overdue.
M ostly we don't do it,
E ven when we want to,
W hy kids do it I don't know!
O ver and over again we are told to do it,
'R eally,' my teachers says to us
'K ids, whatever will you do next?'

Bukky Balogun (9)
St Francesca Cabrini Primary School

JORDANNE

J ordanne is
O pen-minded
R ich, loves the
D eep blue sea
A lways friendly
N ormal
N ever rude and I am sometimes
E xtravagant

Jordanne Joseph (8)
St Francesca Cabrini Primary School

WHEN I'M HAPPY

When my brother plays with me I'm happy.
When my dad carries me around I'm happy.
When my friends play with me I'm happy.
When my brother makes me laugh I'm happy.
When I play with my dad I'm happy.

Wilfredo Padilla (9)
St Francesca Cabrini Primary School

ALL ABOUT ME

S arah is
A lways friendly
R espectful
A nd likes to read,
H as two helpful brothers and

M akes lots of friends.

Sarah Mills (8)
St Francesca Cabrini Primary School

LEANNE

L eanne is funny.
E veryone likes her.
A lways friendly.
N obody hates her.
N ever grumpy.
E veryone knows her.

Leanne Williams-Leonce (9)
St Francesca Cabrini Primary School

CATS

Cats drive me crazy
They are lunatics
And they are not listening to my orders
They scratch me
When my friend came they scratch them too
They try to go to the kitchen so they can get their food
My mum and dad like them better than me.

Arnold Lomboto (8)
St Francesca Cabrini Primary School

BOREDOM IS . . .

Boredom is when you have to read.
Boredom is when you wash up.
Boredom is when you have to work.
Boredom is when there is nothing on TV.
Boredom is when you have to watch TV.
Boredom is when it is raining.
Boredom is when you have to listen.
Boredom is when you have to watch Teletubbies.
Boredom is when you tidy up.

Rosina Ruggeri (7)
St Francesca Cabrini Primary School

HAPPINESS

Happiness is when the sun is shining.
Happiness is when it's your birthday.
Happiness is when you go to a party.
Happiness is when you play with your friends.
Happiness is when you go to the park.
Happiness is when you get a pet.
Happiness is when you get a book.
Happiness is when you get new shoes.
Happiness is when you get sleep.

Okoji Atutu (8)
St Francesca Cabrini Primary School

MY BOOK

Once there was a book,
When I opened it, it shook,
When I shut it, it was still,
It was written with a magic quill.

The name was Magic,
It was tragic,
I threw it in the bin,
It was only thin.

Andrew White (9)
St Francesca Cabrini Primary School

NEVER NEVER NEVER ~ BROKEN PROMISES

I asked my friend to come and play, she said, 'Yes.'
Never never never.
I asked my friend to stay at my house for a night. Her mum said, 'Yes.'
Never never never.
I asked my friend to help me with my work, she said, 'Yes.'
Never never never.
I asked my friend to help me make a cake, she said, 'Yes.'
Never never never.

Chioma Nwachukwu (8)
St Francesca Cabrini Primary School

FRIENDS

My friend drives me crazy,
My friends call me names,
They bully me all day long,
But I just sing my song,
I don't hurt you,
And you don't hurt me,
I will help you,
If you help me,
So we can be good.

Ryan Tucker (9)
St Francesca Cabrini Primary School

DISAPPOINTMENT IS . . .

Disappointment, disappointment is when I get into trouble.
Disappointment, disappointment is homework.
Disappointment, disappointment is when it is raining.
Disappointment, disappointment is when it's home time.
Disappointment, disappointment is being sick.
Disappointment, disappointment is when I am sad.
Disappointment, disappointment is when somebody calls me a name.
Disappointment, disappointment is when the ball goes over the fence.
Disappointment, disappointment is maths.

Branden Dublin (8)
St Francesca Cabrini Primary School

THE WORLD

The world is green, blue and red
All full of beautiful colours come out
And the colours of the world will fulfil you
The green, blue and red.
Come out and see what interesting colours
You will be able to see.

Monike Bartley-Williams (11)
St Francesca Cabrini Primary School

I'M FEELING LONELY

Whenever I am lonely someone is there for me.
Whenever I am lonely I can see.
Whenever I am lonely there's a bee around me.
Whenever I am lonely I think about RE.
Whenever I am lonely there's no light shining in me.

Oyinlola Payne (8)
St Francesca Cabrini Primary School

ANGER IS . . .

Anger is when people kick me.
Anger is when I want to watch TV but I have to go to bed.
Anger is when I can't play games.
Anger is when I have to do homework.
Anger is when it's my birthday but I have to wait till tomorrow.
Anger is when the ball goes over the fence.
Anger is when people throw my shoe over the fence.
Anger is when people hurt me.
Anger is when I am playing and people spoil it.
Anger is when people push me into the fence.

Ryan Roche (7)
St Francesca Cabrini Primary School

BOREDOM IS . . .

Boredom is doing nothing.
Boredom is doing homework.
Boredom is watching Bob the Builder.
Boredom is doing the laundry.
Boredom is doing the ironing.
Boredom is doing my work that my mum gives me.
Boredom is watching 'Honey I Shrunk The Kids' 20 times.
Boredom is hearing Harry Potter tales.
Boredom is being in the car too long.
Boredom is doing handwriting.

James Ogunyale (7)
St Francesca Cabrini Primary School

PIZZA, POEM, POEM, PASTA

Pizza, Pie, Pasta . . .
I need to keep on track, poem, poem, P-Pa pasta, pasta.
This is the difficulty you see, with me
To keep on course of what lies before me.
But my thoughts are stopped by friends called Head and Tummy.
They talk to each other without the Hand knowing.
About why I can't write much further
Because my belly is growling.
My concentration is low and my thoughts are waning.
I need to take my stomach to food storage training.
I pull Head, Hand and Tummy together
So we can work in time.
So we can stay on the topic,
Of writing the next line . . .
Roses are Red,
Violets are Blue,
I'll love you if I could have some stew.
No! That's not right, Head you have lead me adrift.
I thought you were on my side, how can I mend this rift?
Hand, what do you say while you're waiting for words?
Eating! What do you think, I'm not a nerd.
Ice cream, apple pie and lemon curd.
Pizza, lemonade, isn't that why tummy's were made?
Hand don't fail me now, how about my poem?
Oh I give up. Let's get some chow.

Neka Nwachukwu (10)
St Francesca Cabrini Primary School

THE SUN

The sun is playing hide-and-seek,
I screamed and screamed until I leak,
I finally found him screaming and running,
Him the sun was having fun,
We played and played for we were done,
It came the time to say hooray,
The day had come has played,
It's time to take the land of nod,
The sun himself has nodded off far away,
And soon the day was replayed.

Tina McGarvey (10)
St Francesca Cabrini Primary School

ANCIENT EGYPTIANS

A ncient Egyptians were nomads
N ile was where they lived
C autiously they crept about
I n the desert north and south
E ntering the pyramids, looking around
K Nocking on the wall without a sound
T utankhamun was very famous indeed

E ven though he was 16
G ods were very important
Y es important indeed
P apyrus was their paper
T he colour was brown
I ncense was in the sarcophagus
A mazing pieces of gold
N ight-time in the desert
S tars shone on the Sphinx.

Samantha Spicer (9)
St Olave's School

DREAM JOURNEY

Tomorrow I'm going to Egypt
To see all the wonderful sights
I'm going there tomorrow
But now it's time to put out the light
I'm dreaming, I'm dreaming of all the beautiful things
Like Rameses' works of art
Of all the beautiful things
To which he devoted his heart
Of all the beautiful things
There were pyramids that stood tall and bold
Or sarcophagi encrusted with gold
They shimmered so bright in the darkening light
Of all the beautiful things.

Tom Bentley (10)
St Olave's School

THE NILE

On the banks of the Nile
The water is glowing
As excitedly Tutankhamun watches.
Hieroglyphics on papyrus paper
Tutankhamun enjoys reading while the river flows.
Tutankhamun looks over the other side
To see the nomads wander.
The pyramids stand proudly
Shimmering in the moonlight.
The pharaohs guard this amazing sight.
The Nile, The Nile, The Nile!

Jessica Farthing (10)
St Olave's School

THE TOMBS

The Nile shimmered as the sun came up
I cautiously entered the tomb of Tutankhamun
I felt a chill run down my spine as I began to climb
The gods were watching me
I said, 'Stop looking at me,' but they still watched me

The desert was hot as I walked along the banks of the Nile
I peered into another mysterious, gloomy, eerie tomb
But it wasn't Tutankhamun's
While I watched from above I saw the Sun God
As I rowed my boat the Nile, it seemed to go on for miles
I stared at the papyrus reeds
The sun began to do gown
What a lovely day in Egypt.

Jordan Santos-Sindes (9)
St Olave's School

FIVE THOUSAND YEAR OLD EGYPTIANS

A   ncient Egyptians lived in 3000BC.
N   ear the shimmering Nile they decided to settle.
C   rops were difficult to grow in the dry Sahara.
I   nundation suddenly came making farming easier.
E   xcitedly they rejoiced, 'We can grow crops!
N   ow we don't have to worry about starvation.
T   o you O God Hapit, thank you.'

E   at all the food you have harvested.
G   ather the papyrus from the Nile's banks.
Y   oung and delicate shoots will make paper.
P   lant the seeds the way Osiris taught you.
T   each the farming to the young people.

Fraser Wood (10)
St Olave's School

A TRIP TO EGYPT

I
went
to Egypt
for a while
and took a
boat trip down
the Nile. I then went
to see the Sphinx, it
was good to get away from
my sister (who's a minx!)
All the way to a tomb, there
was no light only gloom. When
I went in, camera flashes struck, then
I found out they used to eat duck. The
jewels were very shiny and some were very
tiny. Tutankhamun and Rameses were ancient
Egyptian pharaohs, who were mummified in their tombs,
too bad they didn't have mint Aeros. Just like the ancient
Egyptians I've run out of time because this is the end of my rhyme.

Jack Ashley Stemp (9)
St Olave's School

AUTUMN

The autumn wind flies through the days
Flaming bonfires lit golden red
The transparent dew falls softly
Down on the frosty crisp green grass
The leaves crunch as they burn to ashes
The wood blazes and sparks
Lighting the bright night sky
Gradually the flames die away

Chloe Tuite (9)
St Olave's School

SECRETS OF THE SEA

By the sea it's cool and calm
I dip in my hand and wet my palm
It feels very strange, like a mermaid's scales
It makes me think of old ocean tales
Of dolphins with voices
And sparkling sea horses.

Under the sea there will always be
Treasures to find for you and for me
Great old vessels that in storms were shipwrecked
Hiding many secrets below their decks.

Men in boats and diving suits
Search for wrecks to find their loot
Diamonds and pearls
And plates made of gold
Items from history, precious and old.

Victoria Brinkhurst (9)
St Olave's School

THE MUMMY

In the Sahara a long time ago,
Lived a young king,
Who had everything
But what he wanted most
Was to become a daddy,
Unfortunately he fell ill
With a bad tummy,
Little did he know he would end up
A mummy!

Chloe Hart (9)
St Olave's School

PHARAOHS OF A LOST WORLD

As we entered the lost tomb
My lantern warmed the ancient lying place of lost kings.
Not entered for many ages of old.
Its tiling of gold leaf glimmering in the light.
Still shining through times of past and of the future.
Though the treasures are great
There is a far greater beauty that shines through.
The missing piece of the discovery of a lost time.
Encrypted messages in hieroglyphics pay homage to the god Osiris.
The linen wrapped around the body of old,
Its colour was a shimmering white.
Its leopard skins and treasures of inconceivable beauty
And now ages that it once saw are gone.
If its eyes could see once more
We can only ponder on what they would think.

Jonathan Godwin (10)
St Olave's School

THE TOMB

I entered the tomb of Tutankhamun
To find all of his treasures
And gold beyond all measures
I opened the case
With the gold gleaming face
And hieroglyphics written upon
But what did I see?
A body wrapped in bandages galore
But as I looked more and more
I wondered and wondered about the life before.

James Mundy (10)
St Olave's School

AWESOME WERE THE EGYPTIANS

Awesome were the Egyptians,
Living 3000 years or more.
    Their fabulous gods and pharaohs,
    Like the mighty Osiris who taught them how to farm.
The Nile was a river, boy was it big,
The Nile it glowed, it flowed
But best of all was its inundation each year.
    It was amazing how they wrote,
    The writing was hieroglyphics, boy must it have been hard.
Sahara, what a desert, so large, bigger than England!
Nomads walked through this amazing desert.
    All this evidence is buried deep underground,
Now much of it has been found.
Boy isn't it interesting!

Jake Biggs (10)
St Olave's School

THE GIFT TO THE EGYPTIANS

Its splendour, its greatness flowed across the land,
Flooding the Sahara desert with grace and beauty.
Where the bulrushes sway, in the scented breeze,
The herds chew calmly and graze in the field.
The annual inundation rushes over the valley
Filling it with lovely gifts of crops and seasoning.
A green strip of lush light followed by the gloomy desert of darkness.
The shimmering river sprinkles a whole new life over the Sahara desert.
This long, huge river snaking its own path through a world of nothing.
Turning this sizzling sandy earth into a glowing green gift of life.

Where would this magnificent world be
Without the way of the river Nile!

Jessica Spicer (11)
St Olave's School

ANCIENT EGYPTIANS

A ncient Egyptians lived 5000 years ago,
N ile that flowed so strong and slow.
C enter of attention was the Nile,
I think at the bottom of the Nile there was a silt pile
E nding hunger,
N eeding your riches,
T utankhamun they worshipped you

E ven though your tools were primitive
G etting water was not a problem.
Y oung or bold but still mummies.
P apyrus plants looking beautiful,
T utankhamun pharaoh at the age of nine
I sis, wife of Osiris
A mazingly the
N ile
S till has many secrets to tell.

Shanil Chande (9)
St Olave's School

THE SPHINX

A Sphinx in all its splendour,
Is quite a lovely ancient treasure,
Guarding the path to Giza,
With its treasures older than the leaning Tower of Pisa,
Telling riddles to all men,
But getting no answer from them,
What walks on 4 legs, then 2 legs and finally 3 legs?
A man came from Greece with an answer he knew,
A human, of course, you can tell from the clue.

James Frost (10)
St Olave's School

THE TOMB

As I cautiously enter a majestic pharaoh's tomb,
There is an eerie silence and a glow of gold at the end of the tomb.
So I creep alongside the walls with cryptic clues on them.
When I reached the end of what seemed an everlasting alley,
There are shining silvers, glowing golds, glittering gems
And shimmering sapphires.
The sarcophagus was covered with glowing jewels,
It is as if it is calling, 'Open me, open me!'
So I do what it commands.
All I see is an old rag that is dirty and torn
But once was a fit young pharaoh who ruled Egypt.
I will seal off this tomb till I tell the archaeologists of my discovery.

Lawrence Ash (10)
St Olave's School

THE ANCIENT EGYPTIANS

The ancient Egyptians lived long ago.
The ancient Egyptians lived by the Nile.
The ancient Egyptians wore beautiful jewellery.
The ancient Egyptians wore beautiful clothes.
The ancient Egyptians worshipped lots of gods.
The ancient Egyptians believed in an after life.

They
Buried their
Dead in pyramids
So tall and sealed it
All up behind a wall.

Christopher Hangartner (9)
St Olave's School

ALL ABOUT EGYPT

The Sahara desert is filled with sand,
And nomadic tribes first discovered this land.

In the tombs the lights are dim,
And Osiris had a brother who hated him.

Tutankhamun was a king at the age of nine,
And all the pyramids were built so fine.

The Nile, the longest river in this nation,
Its flooding process called inundation.

When kings and queens of Egypt died,
Their bodies then were mummified.

The air is humid in the day,
To keep them cool they made their houses out of clay.

Fish and bread were their main diet,
The bread had sand and stones in it.

After thousands of years in this great land,
The great Egyptian pyramids still stand.

Jack Read (10)
St Olave's School

OSIRIS

O ld Osiris that king had a nasty brother,
S eth was his unattractive name.
I n only a day Seth was
R id of his brother. But
I sis and the young god Anubis, brought him back to life.
S o Horus, their son, defeated old Seth and became the ruler of Egypt.

Robert Durham (9)
St Olave's School

THE ANCIENT EGYPTIANS

The ancient Egyptians are so cool
But their jewellery was so very small.

While the Nile does inundation
The ancient Egyptians will be enjoying relaxation.

In that tomb Osiris lies
While his fourteen pieces grow twice the size.

The papyrus oh so very old
All of their jewellery was made of gold.

The tops of the pyramids are called the tips
But I don't think they had a solar eclipse.

The Sahara desert is sizzling hot
Killing their animals, what a shot.

Their slaves were so very strong
But the stench of the tombs was a pong.

George Ryan-Smith (10)
St Olave's School

EGYPTIANS

E   gyptians they're amazing and awesome
G   reat artists and sculptors they were
Y   ou never know their tombs could be haunted
P   haraohs had very dark hair
T   he Egyptians quickly learned to plant crops by the River Nile
I   n pyramids there lived lots of scarabs who ran round mummies
    at night
A   pharaoh named Osiris became one of the gods
N   omadic tribes travelled to Giza where pyramids are now found

Byron Harris (9)
St Olave's School

EGYPTIAN HISTORY

The ancient Egyptians are very old
And a lot of their pharaohs' things are made of gold.

All of them have died
And most of them have been mummified.

Inside the pyramids it really stinks
But to get your mind off it you can go and see the Sphinx.

If you're bored you can go to the Nile,
But you can't walk along all of it because it's a lot longer than a mile.

They used to write in hieroglyphics
And they could have been around a lot longer but that's a myth.

Egypt is a great place to be
But it's not as good if you don't like history!

Oliver Price (10)
St Olave's School

THE SAHARA DESERT

Sizzling in the sensational Sahara sun,
Scorching scorpions lie in the settlements of silent nomads,
Noiselessly, they slide across the glowing sandy surface into

their homes,
An oasis served superbly as a home,
Proudly, the nomad leader strode out of his tent,
His camel bowing down majestically for his master to mount,
Unsteadily he rode off towards the Nile,
Towards a new land,
This land - Egypt.

David Ireland (10)
St Olave's School

TUTANKHAMUN

Who could have thought,
This desolate landscape could hold such splendour?
That was only opened less than 80 years ago.
The gold of his mask, glinting in the sun like stars at night,
Carrying the crook and flail,
Representing the shepherd leading the people of Egypt.
The blue eyes on the outer case of his coffin,
Like jewels staring up at the gods.
His tomb was one of few not to have the hundreds upon hundreds
Of the gold items stolen by merciless thieves
Who don't care how they have disrupted history.
The young king,
The youngest king,
Tutankhamun.

Lucas Tuite (10)
St Olave's School

LOST SECRETS

We work in the sun, it is burning us
Glowing as if it wants to hurt us,
Our mission is to find a long lost piece of ancient Egyptian history,
What lies beneath this mysterious desert? What is to be found?
At last a brick, another, some more,
We dig until we can dig no more
A pyramid lies in the lonely desolate landscape,
My heart is racing,
I am impatient, what a magnificent pyramid.
The cryptic sensation lurks beneath me,
What lost secrets are to be learned, what lies in the pyramid?
The lost secrets of ancient Egypt.

Kirsty Pruce (11)
St Olave's School

OSIRIS LIVES!

Osiris was a marvellous king,
All his royal subjects loved him.
He loved his wife Isis, unlike any other,
Only one person hated him
And that was Seth, his brother.

Seth, as I told you hated Osiris,
He would have liked to crush him into papyrus.
He had the head of an unknown beast you see,
And he was jealous of his brother, obviously.

So he plotted a plan with his evil mind
And plucked up all the courage that he could find.
Then he went to the banks of the River Nile,
And waited there for a little while.

Osiris came along for his morning stroll,
Then chop! Chap! Off his arms did roll.
Slish! Slash! Off went his legs,
Thud! *Kersmash!* Off flew his head.

He left him there for a day and a night
All the kingdom was in fright.
But his loving wife Isis, searched near and far,
As low as the ground, as high as a star.

When she found the final part,
She said, 'I'll stick on his legs for a start.'
So she got the body and stuck on his legs.
Put on his arms, glued on his head.

Meanwhile, naughty old uncle Seth,
Battled his nephew Horus until death.
Horus' eyes were plucked from his head, but as last, hoorah,
Seth was dead.

He went to the land of the Underworld,
Good old Horus was King.
The Pharaoh, the champion, Hooray, hurrah
And everyone was happy again.

Janek Newman (10)
St Olave's School

HARRIET

When I was small,
I had a friend at school.
When we went to the park,
We had such a lark.
She had ice cream
All round her mouth
Like the sun at its brightest beam.

In the garden next door
We watched a bonfire,
We spied on men as they threw on trees.

Then one day she moved away
Only photos were left
And a broken heart.

When she moved away
The very next day
I sat in the playground and wept.
I sat in a dark cave
Of sadness, alone.

Amy Errington (8)
St Olave's School

THE PYRAMID

The pyramid was only a couple of strides away
Riding on a camel
The bumpy feeling like a roo in its mum's pouch
The blazing hot sun shining on the pyramid
As soon as I crept in the air went cold
And a sudden chill ran through my body
I crept through looking at all the pictures of the powerful pharaoh
That, 5000 years ago, people worshipped and loved
I stumbled, only to find a magnificent figure of a bird
Layered with dust under a pair of gold wings
Like the gold from a crown, the glowing blue blending in
The two red rubies like great big cherries at either end
I put it back down and left.

Charlotte Ubels (11)
St Olave's School

THE JOURNEY

A   sizzling Sahara desert,
N   ext to the gleaming River Nile.
C   autiously walking into the pyramids
I   ntending to see the kings.
E   xtremely excited to hold some papyrus
N   ot knowing
T   hat I was going to Luxor

E   xtremely amazed to see the tomb of Tutankhamun
G   reat pharaoh Rameses
Y   et Osiris taught them how to
P   lough.
T   he Egyptians were a great civilisation.

Liam Cleary (9)
St Olave's School

THE DEEP BLUE SEA

The sea is a carpet of light blue
That changes colours in the sunlight
But deep, deep down in the ocean
Where you have to swim with all your might
Anglerfish, swordfish and sharks
Roam the pitch black depths
And these fish are very fierce
So they're not to be kept as pets!

But one fish dwarfs them all
The undisputed king of the sea
With an eye as big as a dish
Not the beautiful whale who eats plankton for tea!
This is a fish of enormous size,
Big in every way
As heavy as a forty ton dinosaur
It's the whale shark, not a creature you see every day!

Dougie Hey (8)
St Olave's School

PYRAMIDS

The three pyramids at Giza were gigantic.
It was spectacular to go inside
Looking at the wonderful pictures they drew to show what they did.
It looks like a tomb inside.
The outside looks like a triangle.
Pyramids are thousands of years old.
They have millions of bricks.
It is wonderful to see the pictures.
Pyramids have paintings of what life was like in Egypt.
It feels creepy when you go inside a pyramid.

Kenrick De Nazareth (10)
St Olave's School

DAYDREAMING

Mrs Blythe thinks I'm reading
But I'm in a haunted castle
Surrounded by darkness, no light, no light
The stairs so high, so high
A step crumpled under my feet
So I run and run till the top was in sight.

Mrs Firmstone thinks I'm doing my sums
But I'm a horse galloping through the forest
Then I see a florist
I poke my head in and get a flower
Then a man comes along with a gun
So I go back to my sum.

Mr Witham, thinks I'm singing
But I'm singing with A1
In front of millions of people
Instead of the school.

Sophie Warner (9)
St Olave's School

PYRAMIDS

P   eople dying
Y   oung or old
R   ameses the king
A   man with gold
M   ummified and buried
I   n the Valley of the Kings
D   ug up by villains
S   ome stole his things

Jake Mallen (9)
St Olave's School

DEEP BLUE SEA

Spread of deep blue water
Splashing with fear
Crystal blue blanket
Glowing in the sunlight

Look under the sea
And you will find
Mysterious things in your mind
Like mermaids swimming
To far off lands

And sunning themselves
Upon the sand
Dolphins shining
Starfish whining
What a beautiful place to be
Under the deep blue sea!

Tiffany Francis (9)
St Olave's School

THE DEEP BLUE SEA

The galloping waves,
Rise like peaks in the sunlight,
On the crystal carpet of blue.

The sunset glows crimson,
Behind rocky white cliffs,
Like snowy mountains.

The dolphins swim gracefully,
In the sparkling stretch of sea,
Beyond the forbidding caves.

Joseph Smith-Sands (9)
St Olave's School

DAYDREAM

Mrs Firmstone thinks I'm reading,
But I'm a raven, soaring over an endless city
Dodging lime fumes from dirty factories
To the wonderful countryside, with its fresh green grass.

Mr Schaller thinks I'm jogging,
But I'm a tiger prowling on my land
Baring my teeth with every growl I make
My claws stab the ground and pierce every living beetle.

Mrs Blythe thinks I'm writing,
But I'm a cat curled around on a comfy rug,
Warming up in front of the fire,
Gently purring as I flex my paws.

Mr Whitham thinks I'm singing,
But I'm a dragon roaming the plains
Blasting jets of fire into the clear breeze,
Searching out victims to roast with a single breath.

Rachel Sesu (9)
St Olave's School

THE MYSTERIOUS MUMMY

As I sneaked into the tomb, it was a wondrous palace
Jewels everywhere I turned
But there standing in the corner was the grey and dull mummy
Wrapped in linen with no sarcophagus
It was an unknown king, its tomb had been stolen by thieves long ago
Fortunately the jewels hadn't been taken
All the glimmering gold stunned me
Then when I turned around
The mummy had gone . . .

Jack Ross Rixon (11)
St Olave's School

OVER AND UNDER

A stretch of deep blue water
Light blue sparkling stretch.
Changing colours in the sunlight
A crystal blue blanket.

Beyond pitch black foreboding caves
With rocky cliffs behind.
The sea looks quite magical
When the sun's gleaming down on the tide.

I love sitting on the nice warm sand
Watching the crabs walk by.
Feeling the waves lapping my toes
And hearing seagulls cry.

Dolphins jumping high in the air
Fish swimming without a care.
Stingrays and lobsters
At the bottom of the sea.
The sea is a wonderful place to be.

Sam Elliott (9)
St Olave's School

THE MUMMY

It just lies there so white
All wrapped up in linen bandages.
The lid of the tomb is magnificently decorated
With patterns reflecting the look of the mummy inside!
I stand wondering what his eyes had seen.
Once so important,
But now tucked away in the gloomy, dark pyramid
Where no one will see him again.

Sara Taylor (10)
St Olave's School

MY FRIEND

My friend is a wonderful friend
He follows me around like a dog
He is a really fun playmate
He finds secret places and passages
We race up and down the long sloping playground.

One weekend we went to the zoo
We ate sandwiches and chocolate bars
In the adventure playground
We swung on the bars like monkeys
When my friend drove away I sulked
I went to a corner - alone.

I'll never forget the day my friend left
But still have some memories
A photograph stands in the hallway
His eyes look at me as I pass
He writes to me in the spring
And although he is no longer there
I will always remember . . .

My friend.

Joseph Newman (8)
St Olave's School

RAIN SONG

I watched the rain bounce off my rooftop,
Plop onto the wet, grey pavement.

Getting more and more angry.
Splashing, thumping, splattering.
Beating at frightened trees.

Toby Ballentyne (8)
St Olave's School

SEA FEVER

A crystal blanket of sea water,
Shimmering in the sunlight,
Changing golden, blue and white,
Seagulls crying out.

Under the water are magical things,
Dolphins singing and mermaids swimming.
Sea horses swim elegantly,
Jumping fish glide through the air.

In rock pools are starfish red and blue,
Sea shells coloured with imagination,
Spiky anemones enjoying their relaxation,
Beyond the sun-yellow sand.

Jennifer Emm (8)
St Olave's School

THE SUNSHINE BEACH

The spread of the deep blue water.
The changing colours of the rocky cliffs
Of white crumbly chalk.
Pitch black threatening caves lie underneath.

The deep blue sea is a crystal blue blanket.
A light sparkling stretch
Lies against the bright yellow sand.

The changing colour of the rocky cliff
Turns to choppy grey.
The shells are buried in the carpet of sand.

Carl Foster (8)
St Olave's School

A STORMY SEA

The captain stood in his cabin,
Looking over the view of the waves,
All blue and green together,
As calm as could be.
Alas, the captain was worried,
For further out to sea,
Was a great big gale,
Which would be the end
Of his crew and him.

On went the little ship,
The Princess Ann she was called,
On into the gale, into the swirling wind,
Into the choppy water,
The wind like a knife
That had been sharpened yesterday
By a metal worker and his wife.
As they fought with the ropes and sail,
The lookout saw a sight,
A lobster ship turned over,
The lookout thought he might
Try and rescue her.

The Princess Ann sailed on,
Past Lisbon, past Paris
And into the grey English Channel.
The captain was sad,
His heart was full of sorrow,
He had seen many wonderful sights,
But was tired and would rest tomorrow.

Alistair Wooder (9)
St Olave's School

MY BEST FRIEND

My best friend,
Was one in a million,
She got ten out of ten every day,
We thought our friendship would never end,
Until the day,
That fateful day,
We found she would have to move.

It seemed like our string of friendship,
Had been cut,
The day she moved was stormy,
Inside and out,
I walked through the rain,
To the house next door,
For the last time,
To give her a fond farewell.

Kathleen Spriggs-Bush (9)
St Olave's School

WHEN THE RAIN COMES

The street is wet
The gutters are full
The rain fires down from thundering clouds
Umbrellas come up
Rain gushes down
Drops explode as they shoot from the clouds
Pounding rain thumps on my roof.

Jamie Kitchener (9)
St Olave's School

FOAM WHITE HORSES

Foam White Horses dance about
On the shores of East Australia
While surfers surf and divers dive
Those horses seem alert, alive

Some mermaids swim and others ride
Foam White Horses quite alive
Foam White Horses prance and dance
But never do they sleep

In stormy weather, they rage and toss
And buck and kick with all their might
But when the weather's calm again
They rest once more in the bright sunlight
Those Foam White Horses

Joseph Rock (8)
St Olave's School

MY SEASHELL DREAM

I went to the sea and below my feet
Stood a beautiful smooth seashell.
I lifted it to my ear to see
If I could hear the song it may tell.
I listened away for a year and a day
But then it was time to go
And when I got home, quiet and alone
I rested it on my pillow.

I dreamt of ocean tales from long, long ago
And whales like kings under the waves below
    In my seashell dream.

Holly Stratton (8)
St Olave's School

THE SPLENDOURS OF EGYPT

The baking sun whipped the backs of slaves,
Water glistened in the River Nile but not a drop
Would cleanse the dry mouths of those who worked so hard,
The towering pyramids of Giza, the masterful Sphinx,
Such beauties that dot the Earth were built in a barren, desolate desert,
Carved, sculptured and built by the hands of amateurs,
And later some of these pyramids shall be filled with bodies
Wrapped in bandages, anointed with the sweetest of scents,
They shall ascend to the god Osiris' domain
Within their subjects' creations and with their subjects' blessing.

Louise Hawkins (10)
St Olave's School

THE MUMMY

It lay there in its robe of ghostly white
I wondered what treasures its eyes had previously seen
Once a pharaoh ruling the land so high above the rest
Now forgotten and lying gathering layers of fine dust
Deserted and desolate, alone
Yet mysterious and secretive, surrounded by cryptic clues
I could see it, how it had been, adorned with garments of fine cloth
And precious jewels that caught the light
But that is the past and this is now
And today it lies in rags of old . . .
    The mummy.

Georgina Stroud (10)
St Olave's School

RAINY DAYS

Pitter patter the rain spits down
Sprinkling, it begins to get wet
Plot, a droplet drops down
Splash, then more.
Suddenly it's pouring!
Rain shoots and explodes
Then it trickles
Spits, dripping
Then stops.

Angus Mair (8)
St Olave's School

RAINY DAY

When the rain blows
It goes pitter patter pitter patter
It goes on the ground
Bang, bang
The sound of drumming outside
Hissing and pounding on my roof.

Jack May (8)
St Olave's School

RAIN SONG

Splatter, tap went the rain,
On a winter's night,
The teardrops fall and cry
On my bedroom window.

As I look out at the exploding teardrops,
Falling from the daring sky,
I see the wet pavement,
Shining and glistening.

Luke Mortimer (8)
St Olave's School

WHEN THE RAIN FALLS

Rain splatters on rooftops.
Rain trickles on umbrellas.
Suddenly hats go up, umbrellas fly high.
Gutters fill, start to leak, dripping on the floor.
Thunder crackles.
Crackle, bang, crackle, bang, rain pours.
The storm fades and goes.
Boys and girls come out to play.

Reece Clifford (8)
St Olave's School

RAIN SONG

Splish, splash falls the rain
Thump onto my roof.
I go outside and I get soaked.
It looks angrily at me
Hitting at my face.
The rain keeps coming down harder,
Harder it tumbles,
Beating and hitting on my house.

Lauren Daley (8)
St Olave's School

RAINY DAYS

I hate rainy days
It makes me very wet
I can't take my dog for a walk
Not even another pet.
It pats on my rooftop and knocks on my front door
I have to look outside in case there's any more.
At night it thunders, it wakes me up.
The rain pours, hisses and rushes down.

Alex Daley (8)
St Olave's School

THE HARD RAIN

Trickling, dripping rain to the ground
It's getting stronger hissing around
Banging droplets on the window sill
The rain pounds through the winter night
The rain has faded away
So in the morning I can say
It's sunny again after a long stormy night.

Stephanie Hollingsworth (7)
St Olave's School

RAIN SONG

Trickle, tap goes the rain
On my plastic cat flap.
It falls in showers
Onto the solid pavement.

Cars speed through the splattering rain,
Drumming on their tin roofs.
The rain is calming down.
The clouds stop crying.

Jack Crowe (8)
St Olave's School

STOPPING STARTING RAIN

Pitter patter the rain pours down
The umbrellas come up,
The streets get wet
Cars send spray flying into the air
The thunder strikes
The people outside hurry home
Then they step out again.

Hugo Humphreys (7)
St Olave's School

WHEN RAIN FALLS

Pitter patter pitter patter
Clouds are coming.
The rain is pouring down
Umbrellas are coming up.
The rain is pounding on the ground.
The clouds are going black.
Rain is crashing on the umbrellas.

Lewis Davey (7)
St Olave's School

ANCIENT EGYPT

They came years and years ago,
They settled aside of the Nile's flow.
They grew their crops from the inundation,
And soon there became an Egyptian nation.
They travelled from high, they travelled from low,
Egypt was where they wanted to go.
It was a marvellous country they had picked,
We now know it as ancient Egypt.

William Sutcliffe (11)
St Olave's School

RAIN SONG

Clouds throw the sky's teardrops down in torrents.
It slaps the beautiful pavement
Quickly kissing it.

It wallops the solid, hard floor.
The teardrops softly fall on my bedroom window
Exploding on the shiny ground.

Richie Barclay (8)
St Olave's School

RAIN SONG

Today I looked out of my window,
And I saw trickling down
Raindrops like children's teardrops,
Looking like the clouds were crying.

People drenched from head to toe,
As the rain hits them,
It explodes on their heads,
And bounces off umbrellas.

Elizabeth Evans (8)
St Olave's School

RAIN SONG

Trickle tinkle,
That's how the rain splashes,
Teardrops fill the sky,
And kiss the twinkling pavement.

The street gets filled with silver paint,
And cars go thundering through.

Nicola Durham (7)
St Olave's School

RAIN SONG

Rain falls like a fountain
Pitter patter
Splash and splatter.

Rain falls like a waterfall
Tapping, trickling
Hitting and beating.

Mica Berditch (7)
St Olave's School

RAIN SONG

The rain thunders down
From the dark, dark sky
It bounces off car rooftops.

The clouds throw torrents of rain
Rapidly down
As it taps on the window
It wants to come in.

The tinkling rain comes
Sprinkling, shooting down.

It constructs immense puddles
Drops explode and scatter down the road.

Philip Smith (8)
St Olave's School

RAINDROPS

Pounding, crashing goes the rain
Outside my window, it really is a pain.
The rain keeps going.
The rivers keep flowing.
I never thought I would see the day
When the sun would see the day
When the hissing and spitting would end.
But - hey look - the sun, the sun
So everyone goes out to have some fun.

Amy Stock (8)
St Olave's School

THE STORM

Thundering, hitting with all its might.
Clouds banging in the night.
Rain falls on the rooftops.
Splashing high.
They land on the ground.
Jumping high.

Frankie Lee (8)
St Olave's School

RAINDROP

When the rain hits the ground
I hear a sprinkling sound.
When the rain hits my window
I hear a hissing sound.
When the rain hits the roof
It bangs really hard.

Olivia Board (7)
St Olave's School

THE LIGHTNING

Splattering, pattering on the windowpane.
Crash, bang, boom, splash!
That's how the thunder goes
Clouds spitting down rain on the muddy grass.
Hear the rain settling calm and still.

Oscar Aragones (7)
St Olave's School

RAINY DAY

Clouds are black
Rain crashing on windows
The gutters are full
Everything is wet
The clouds are grey
The rain gushes down on rooftops
Bounces off the pavement
The clouds go white
Rain plops to the ground
And trickles away.

William Hunter (7)
St Olave's School

RAIN SONG

I watch the rain
Thumping on the ground
Like an angry waterfall.

Slapping on the big hard floor,
I watch the crows soaring to their nests
Flying to safety from the rain
That is coming down in torrents.

George Dickinson (7)
St Olave's School